I E CAHN
860 5TH AV
NEW YORK N Y
    10021

RODERICK CAMERON

SHELLS

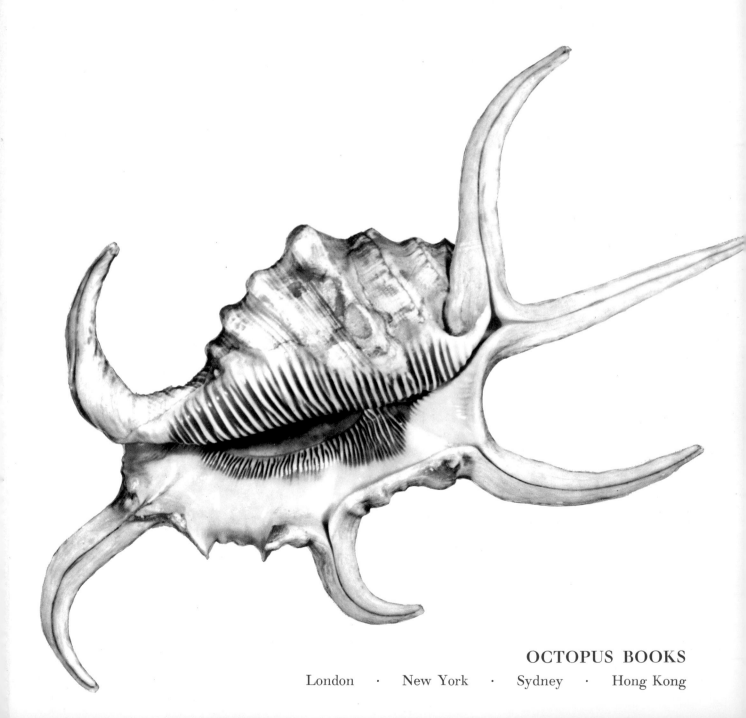

OCTOPUS BOOKS

London · New York · Sydney · Hong Kong

Acknowledgments

Photographs numbers 21, 23, 25 appear by courtesy of the National Portrait Gallery, London, and number 26 by courtesy of the Ashmolean Museum, Oxford. Numbers 35 and 13 are by permission of *Connaissance des Arts* (photographs by A. Dingjan, The Hague). Number 44 is reproduced by courtesy of the Linnean Society, numbers 110, 114 by courtesy of the Agent-General for Queensland and number 39 by courtesy of the Royal Botanic Gardens, Kew. Number 7 appears by courtesy of *L'Oeil* and number 115 by permission of the Victoria and Albert Museum, London. Numbers 6, 29, 30 are by Claude Michaelides, number 11 by Photographie Giraudon, number 8 by Shell Photographic Unit and number 16 by A. E. Coe and Sons, Norwich. All the other photographs were taken by John R. Freeman, from the collections in the British Museum, the British Museum of Natural History (and are reproduced by the permission of the Trustees) and from the author's collection. The author wishes to thank Mrs St George Saunders and Mr S. P. Dance for their invaluable assistance

Preceding page
Specimen of *Lambis rugosa*
from the Red Sea

This edition first published 1972 by
OCTOPUS BOOKS LIMITED
59 Grosvenor Street, London W.1

ISBN   7064 0032 1

© **1961 by Roderick Cameron**

PRODUCED BY MANDARIN PUBLISHERS LIMITED AND PRINTED IN HONG KONG

Shells in Art

1 *Murex monodon*

WALKING ON THE EDGE of the sea along the luminous margin that divides land from water, which of us, if he notices a shell at his feet, is not tempted to stoop and pick it up? Shells have fascinated men of every period; and I remember myself how, in my childhood, I spent hours hunting for the little white-ribbed cowries so plentiful on English beaches. My governess called them 'pig cowries'; but in my mind they evoked a very different kind of image—each shell suggested the rosy, henna-stained finger-tips of some celestial houri. I did not divulge my ideas

2 *Turritella duplicata*

3 An engraving of *Cypraea erosa* from Martin Lister's *Historia Conchyliorum*

to Miss Sheriff, who would, no doubt, have disapproved; and, silently, occupied with our own thoughts, we went our separate ways across the sand. By the end of the summer months I had amassed a fairly large collection; and these early experiences may perhaps have encouraged me, many years later, to pay a visit to the Australian Great Barrier Reef, which, together with the Philippines, is probably the richest shell-producing area of the world.

My impressions of these tropical seas, however, will be dealt with elsewhere. First, I must try to paint a broader picture, and show, for instance, the important part that shells have played as a source of inspiration in the creative arts. I must also attempt to outline the history of shell collecting, and describe how it grew from the concern of a few naturalists to a serious science housed in national museums. Finally, I should like to give some details of the shells themselves, choosing the rarer varieties, or those shells which have some arresting peculiarities.

The early nineteenth-century naturalist, George Perry in *Conchology*, 1811, remarks that 'The study of shells is a branch of natural history which, although not greatly useful to the mechanical arts, or the human economy, is nevertheless, by the beauty of the subjects it comprises, most admirably adapted to recreate the senses, to improve the state of invention of the artist'. Certainly, it is easy to trace the part shells have played as a source of inspiration in the creative arts. Even primitive man, at the end of the last Ice Age, was conscious of the beauty of natural objects, and appreciated nature's creations long before he began to create himself. In the limestone caverns of France and Belgium, numerous remains of shells have been found, pierced with holes so that they could be attached to some pieces of clothing. From classical antiquity to the present day, the shell appears as a decorative motif in ornament, architecture and sculpture. But the form in which it is employed varies greatly. The Egyptians, for instance, used it in jewellery alone, and produced stylized golden cowries, the underside of the shell showing the teeth. In one example which dates from the Middle Kingdom, about 2000 BC, gold shells are threaded alternately with pale amethyst beads, to form a short necklace. During the period of the New Kingdom, when there was a trend towards naturalism, real shells were used again, cowries, as well as small cones and plaques of mother-of-pearl. The 'Men-of-the-Isles', as the Minoans were called by the

4 The *Cardium pseudolima* or Giant cockle, from West Africa

5 *Biplex perca* or Finned frog

6 (*opposite*) Frontispiece from *La Conchyliologie* by Dezallier d'Argenville, Paris, 1757, from a drawing by Boucher

Egyptians, also used various shells as decorative motifs, but far more extensively than the Egyptians. This is hardly surprising, since they were a seafaring people who worshipped the Great Mother and other divinities who held sway over the sea. Shells carpeted the floor of her palace. One finds wine jars decorated with octopuses, their tentacles treated like the tendrils of a vine, interlacing the volutions of a graceful shell. There are clay Minoan drinking cups, decorated with raised cockle shells; and alabaster representations of the conch have been found in the various necropolises. On the walls of Minos' palace, bare-breasted, wasp-waisted priestesses are depicted sounding conch-horns; and Crete provides yet another example; a large *Tonna* or white tun shell cut out of volcanic glass.

From Crete we pass on to Greece and Aphrodite, Goddess of Desire, rising naked from the foam within an open scallop shell. Aphrodite means 'foam-born'; and, according to the legend, she first stepped ashore on the Island of Cythera, but, finding it too small, passed on to the Peloponnese, and eventually took up residence at Paphos on the western tip of Cyprus, which was to remain the principal seat of her worship.

There, every spring, the priestesses bathed themselves in the sea, a rite that purified them of past license. Aphrodite had always been a marine divinity, and shells are among the symbolic attributes found in her temples. Sea urchins and cuttle fish were also sacred to her. The God of the Sea himself, Poseidon, had his underwater palace off Aegea; and Thetis, the Sea Goddess, with her fifty nereids, gentle and beautiful mermaids, was represented much later as surrounded with pearls, shells and sea-grasses [figure 6].

The motif of Aphrodite's birth was a subject particularly suited to the plastic arts; and by Hellenic artists she was represented in small clay figurines, emerging from between the half-open valves of a scallop. When the Romans assimilated the Greek pantheon, and Aphrodite became Venus, we find her in Rome, in mosaics and on murals, again with the scallop. Towards the first century BC, the shell is used as an architectural element. Thanks to its rigid symmetry, the scallop suited Roman taste. The uneven surface and the play of light and shadow divided by the ridges made a perfect motif for the smooth curves of the alcove, and gave the expert Roman engineers an occasion to display their virtuosity.

LA
CONCHYLIO
LOGIE.

8 St James the Apostle in his pilgrim robes, wearing a scallop shell shell attached to the broad brim of his hat. This fifteenth-century statue by Juan de Malines is in St Mary's chapel, Oviedo Cathedral

Early Christian art borrowed the shell motif from antiquity, still using it as a decorative motif, and not apparently as a specific Christian symbol. A chill wind blew from the books of Moses, and Jehovah's injunctions were carefully noted: 'All that have not fins and scales in the seas, and in the rivers, and all that move in the waters, and any living thing which is in the waters, they shall be an abomination unto you'. These warnings, however, did not prevent Christian mosaicists, at work in Rome and Ravenna, from incorporating the shell forms in their alcoves and splendid gold canopies. A good example is the panel of San Vitale that shows the Empress Theodora and her retinue bedecked in a parure of enormous pearls. Theodora stands under the green and red ribbings of a large scallop; and it is interesting to see that the material for the setting of her parure is cut from mother-of-pearl.

During the Middle Ages, the antique shell motif appeared only spasmodically in European art. The harmonious rounded forms that satisfied the architects of Rome and Constantinople were less appreciated in the Gothic north. Thus the shell during this period appears mainly as the badge of the Apostle James, the patron saint of pilgrims [figure 6]. An obscure legend has it that St James had preached in Spain, and the relics of the saint were said to have been discovered during the ninth century by Theodorus, Bishop of Iria, who was guided by a star to the cave which concealed the bones. The town which grew up near this place came to be called Compostella and is on the north-west coast of Spain. Compostella is supposed to be a corruption of *campus stellae*, or 'Plain of the Stars'. The pious, who were in the habit in those days of making pilgrimages on foot to sanctuaries, no longer had access to the Holy Land, now cut off by infidels. Instead, they took the road of a new pilgrim route through France into Spain, over the Pyrenees to the tomb of St James. The first pilgrims, after having paid their respects to the saint, are reported to have gone down to bathe and found the beach strewn with scallop shells, which they decided to take with them as a sign that they had completed their pilgrimage. The scallop thus became an attribute of St James and a token that the pilgrim had visited his shrine. In representations of St James, he is seen wearing a scallop shell attached to the broad brim of his pilgrim hat or on his pilgrim's bag; for from the twelfth century onwards St James is generally represented in pilgrim robes. Santiago

9 Argonaut-shaped porcelain wall-pocket with a purple overlay, by Wedgwood, *c*. 1805

10 *Busycon contrarium*

de Compostella being an important pilgrimage centre of Christendom, the pilgrims felt a certain confidence if they remained true to their promises made at the foot of St James's tomb. In many twelfth and thirteenth-century churches, sculptured scenes of the last judgment show corpses leaving their graves at the summons of the angel's trumpet. Many of them brandish the shell of St James, a protection against the Fiend and his minions who, armed with pitchforks, leer at them out of the flames.

With the coming of the Renaissance the shell reappeared as a common decorative and architectural motif. When taste reverted to antique prototypes, it was natural that the new movement should seize upon the scallop, whose shape so well complemented the Renaissance idea of symmetry. We frequently find a shell appearing as a canopy above Madonna paintings, while sculptors of the period were in the habit of placing their statues in alcoves modelled in the form of shells.

The New Learning brought with it a revival of all the themes of antique mythology. All the deities of the pagan pantheon parade before us, if only as an excuse for the newly discovered cult of the naked human body. An obvious example is Botticelli's *Birth of Venus*, in which the Goddess emerges from a choppy, pale blue sea, borne along on a large scallop. Her barque has just reached the shore and she makes a forward movement that will carry her floating on air above the flower-sprigged ground. Tenderly, she tries to cover herself with her long golden tresses.

In Renaissance and later architecture, we come across frequent examples of the shell motif. Bramante used it in his wonderful Tempietto, hidden away behind a wall of San Pietro in Montorio; Michelangelo also used it constantly. Bernini, in the Piazza Barberini in Rome, presents a Triton riding astride a granite shell, blowing petals of water from a conch which he holds up against the sky; and in the same square, we admire the wide open scallop of the Fontana delle Api.

In Holland, at Antwerp, a whole school of painters was to spring up, artists who specialized in depicting what were called *Cabinets d'Amateurs*. In one canvas there is a gathering of *dilettanti*, elegantly dressed in silks, with ruffs and high hats and embroidered gloves; in another, a man and his wife, attended by a page and his dog, have just walked in through an open door giving on to a formal

11 A seventeenth-century *Cabinet d'Amateur*, painted by Cornelius de Baellius, now in the Louvre

12 *Pecten jacobaeus* or Pilgrim scallop, an engraving from Martin Lister's *Historia Conchyliorum*

garden; the room is high-ceilinged and hung from top to bottom with paintings. All the cabinets depicted by this Antwerp school include a large table, spread with a thick Oriental carpet, on which repose numerous shells [figure 11]. Amongst a plethora of scientific instruments, of globes and astrolabes, we distinguish the pearly shell of a nautilus mounted as a goblet, or a great *Turbo Marmoratus* from the China seas. Other canvases show us cones, volutes and striped and patterned bivalves, large cockles and thorny oysters. What is interesting is the remarkable accuracy with which all these shells are delineated.

The age of Rococo, or *rocaille* style of the eighteenth century, is scattered with shells of every kind, their forms interpreted quite arbitrarily, indeed at times twisted and furled beyond recognition. In the china of the period and in the recently invented porcelain, we come across salts, basins, baskets, dishes and centre-pieces made up of a composition of different varieties of shells. A whole dessert service of Josiah Wedgwood's famous Queen's ware was inspired by the Argonaut [figure 9]; and another dinner service was based on the common cockle, embellished with shells in relief and tinted in different shades of brown. Several of the continental porcelain manufacturers used the various bivalves as patterns. So did the silversmiths.

In this brief review of the part shells have played as a motif in the creative arts, two important developments have been completely ignored: the mounted shell of the sixteenth century and the even earlier shell grottoes. The Renaissance was the golden age of mounted shells, particularly in Germany and Austria. It was the age of the *Schatzkammer* or treasure chamber, when the different ruling houses vied with each other to enhance the splendours of their courts. This taste for luxury flourished in all the capitals of Europe, and along with it came a hankering after the exotic. The sixteenth century was an age to fire men's imagination. The New World had just been discovered; and strange stories were told of a prodigiously wealthy kingdom found in Mexico, of a civilization that dressed in brilliant feathers and ate off gold. There were other vast regions still only guessed at, and new discoveries were constantly being made. The conquistadors brought back with them strange minerals and unknown flowers; and it is hardly surprising that amateurs should have started to collect what were then termed natural curiosities. Shells, of course, figured prominently among these eagerly awaited cargoes. Later, they were to be appreciated for themselves; but for the moment fashion prescribed a more fastidious use of them. The goldsmiths of Europe were kept busy turning out the most complicated mounts, the shells most commonly used being the *Nautilus* and the *Turbo*, often with their outer skins burnt off by acid to expose the nacreous lining. Their shapes, and the fact that both shells possessed a wide lip, made it possible to mount them as drinking goblets; and that is how many of them were presented [figure 13]. Gold and silver dolphins, sea-gods, tritons or mermaids with gem-encrusted tails and enamelled breasts, held aloft a multitude of fragile mother-of-pearl coils. The fragility of the shell was part of the object's charm.

Thanks to the seventeenth-century Dutch and Portuguese navigators, Europe was no longer dependent on the long overland spice routes; and cargoes from the Indies now arrived at Dutch or Hanseatic ports along the Baltic.

13 A mounted *Nautilus pompilius* dating from the first half of the sixteenth century now in the Lazaro Goldiano Museum in Madrid

14 (*opposite*) *Tonna luteostoma* or Tun shell, a copy of a plate from Küster's *Conchylien Cabinet*, Nuremberg, 1857

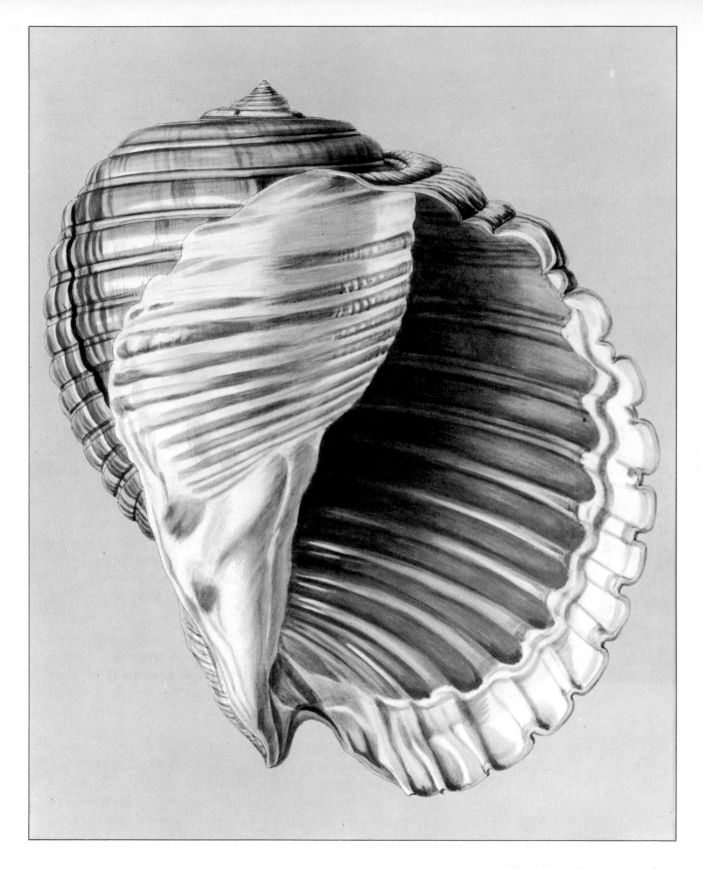

13

15 *Fusus colus*, an engraving from Martin Lister

Hamburg, Stettin and Danzig took the place of Venice; and it is to those cities that we must look for the best examples of mounted shells.

They were not always treated as goblets. Sometimes artists used their shining spirals in other ways, forcing them to represent the convulsed body of a dragon or the elegant form of a swan—employing the same technique, in fact, as jewellers applied to baroque pearls.

Simultaneously with this love of the exotic imports from faraway lands, there sprang up a fashion for building grottoes, or artificial caves, filled with rocks, stones and shells. First they provided shady garden retreats, where it was pleasant to hear the dripping of water over moss-covered stone, and to admire reclining sea-gods framed in stylized stalagmites. The Romans had understood these pleasures, as can be seen from the recently excavated villa at Sperlonga which lies mid-way between Rome and Naples. But the grottoes or shell-rooms that concern us here were begun for the most part in the early eighteenth century and have a more architectural character. Few parks, during the eighteenth century, were without grottoes, temples, or ruins.

At Goodwood Park, in Sussex, stands a very elegant little pavilion entirely lined in shells, used as an architect would use wood or stone or plaster [figure 7]. Three is no trace here of the gloom of a cave or grotto; one enters a charming room in shining colours—white and pink and mauve, picked out elegantly with black. It took the second Duchess of Richmond and her daughters seven years to complete. The Duke also helped in arranging the shells, but his appearances were somewhat intermittent.

There is a pavilion of much the same kind in the royal park of Rambouillet, built by the Duke of Penthièvre for his young daughter-in-law, the Princesse de Lamballe. It is equally precise and entirely architectural, with Ionic pilasters and niches worked in beautifully matched mussels. Water-polished stones in different colours have been used as a mosaic on the floor, and the whole interior glows with a soft mother-of-pearl light.

Until quite recently, before its demolition, one could visit the extraordinary shell grotto at Oatland's Park, where the Duke of York entertained the Emperor of Russia and the other victors of Waterloo to a splendid supper. The walls were heavily encrusted with glistening white spar; and cowries and white and pink shells were

16 Shells, by Jean van Kessel, from the collection of Lt-Col R. C. Allhusen

17 *Tonna galea*, an engraving from Martin Lister's *Historia Conchyliorum*

interspersed with mirrors and crystal sconces, all very cleverly used and applied with great feeling for their decorative qualities. One of the corridors leading to the grotto was entirely lined with the teeth of horses killed on the field of Waterloo.

As Barbara Jones tells us in her excellent book *Follies and Grottos*, there was a period when 'duchesses, bankers and poets gathered shells on the shore, begged them from travellers, scrambled for them at sales and bought whole shipments when they had to. Specimens of minerals, felspars and fossils joined the shells, and the lovely glittering collections, fresh from the sea, not dusty and brown as we see them now, were turned into grottoes. Rooms, caves and whole suites of underground apartments, furnished with baths and marble seats, carpeted with moss for special occasions and tinkling perpetually with cascades, were entirely encrusted with shells and spar in half the great houses in England'.

Many other eighteenth-century shell grottoes might be listed and described; but, as the century approached its end, man's attitude towards nature changed, and scientific interest was combined with romantic admiration. The nineteenth century in the conchological field was the age of the well-informed collector. Shells, crystals and butterflies were to be learnedly catalogued, and dried plants carefully classified in albums. It was left to great-aunts to amuse themselves by sticking winkles and mussels and pig-cowries, the more ordinary shells of our northern shores, into wet plaster, thus forming frames for dressing-table mirrors and lids for trinket boxes. Ships' captains also returned with shells that they had transformed into silver-mounted snuff-boxes. In Dublin I found four tiger cowries which, by judicious cutting and mounting, had been pressed into service as containers for salt and pepper. Some traveller had brought them back for his sister or his betrothed, for, engraved on the silver bands framing them, I read the name 'Dora'.

One of the great commercial concerns of the world, Shell Oil, was founded on this very kind of bric-à-brac. Old Marcus Samuel, the present Lord Bearsted's great-grandfather, had a shop in what was then called Sailors' Town, near the Tower of London. It was a district that catered for the needs of sailors and ships; and old Marcus would buy the sailors' wares, particularly sea-shells from the Far East. With these shells mounted into boxes, he laid the foundations of his business. When he died in 1870, his estate was valued at forty thousand pounds; and it was with the increment of the money he left that the family built the first oil tanker, with which the Samuels were to break down the world monopoly held by Rockefeller and his Standard Oil Company. Out of gratitude to old Marcus, the Company's oil tankers were named after shells, the first being called *Murex*.

So far, we have only dealt with the Mediterranean and European civilizations. No mention has been made of the Americas—the whole vast field of Pre-Columbian art: the Aztec, Toltec, Maya and Inca cultures. They adapted shells and shell motifs in much the same way as did the Cretans and the early Greeks. Before me as I write, I have a baked clay model of the genus *Rostellaria*, probably Toltec. It is stylized but easily recognizable. There is a hole at its apex, and another one about half-way up its spire. Obviously it was used as a whistle. I have seen other representations of shells in different kinds of pottery, and, of course, a great deal of jewellery, including the necklace

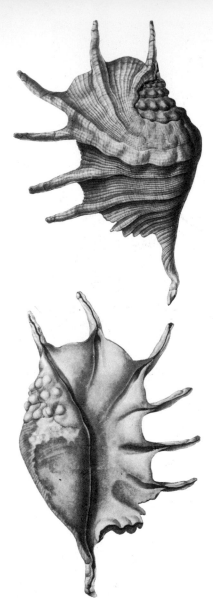

19 Wash-drawing of *Lambis lambis* by Jacques Enstach Desèves, pupil of H. J. Redouté, from an album of original drawings in the British Museum, never previously reproduced

of olive shells in the Bliss Collection, momentarily housed in the National Gallery in Washington. Each individual shell has been drilled through the lip for stringing; and the butt ends have been ground down to expose the interior spiral structure. The collection also includes a gorget of conch shells, every unit having been cut out from the thickest part of the outer curve of the shell. From the north coast of Peru comes an inlaid scallop pendant, showing two gulls with turquoise eyes devouring a fish.

The majority of North-American Indian tribes made use of scallops, or clams; while on the west coast the tribes worked with inlaid abalone shells, and the Chinooks of Oregon ornamented their noses and ears with the *Dentalium* or tooth shells.

Whenever I visit the Ethnological wing of the British Museum, I am always delighted to see the be-feathered and be-shelled world of the South Pacific. The natives of New Caledonia, for example, wear headpieces formed by large white tun shells or *Tonna*, which are kept in place by chin straps of flying-fox fur [figure 14]. From the Gilbert Islands comes a suit of armour consisting of a corselet, an over-shirt and trousers made from heavily plaited strands of coconut fibre; a fish-skin helmet—the prickly skin of a parrot-fish taken at the moment of its distension—covers the head. To complete this strange ensemble, the figure in the British Museum carries a stout wooden sword, the blades of which are completed by an inlay of jagged shark's teeth. The Polynesian exhibits have a quieter look—necklaces of cone shell discs, made from the flat end of the shell, picked out in its natural markings with outward swirling black dots. Coronets of small sea snails are ingeniously strung together to form a four-sided strand; and white chest-plaques have been carved from the shell of a giant clam, squares measuring a yard across, from the Solomon Islands. Other plaques, made to be worn on the forehead, were cut from large pearl shells. Attached to them is an open filigree-work of tortoise-shell, silhouetted against the soft whiteness of the oyster. There was no end to the ingenuity displayed by the Polynesians—necklaces of sea-weed stems and human teeth, or of small mauve limpets, strung in groups of six, interspersed with black polished seeds. In India and Africa, artists have also made ingenious use of shells; and early travel-books describe young girls living on the Coromandel Coast, their arms and ankles encircled from infancy with broad shell

20 *Turris Babylonia*

bands cut from the whorls of the great *Turbinella pyrum*, or sacred chank [figure 115]. Engravings show Sepoy troops wearing necklaces, made from the canal of the same shell, as part of their parade uniform. Throughout the African continent, Negroes once wore *Cypraea moneta*, or money cowry, stitched on to their baskets or clothing [figure 66]. In Ghana, cowries form complicated head-dresses; and in Benin these are inlaid in the pavements of important buildings. In one chief's house, they have been worked into figures depicting a fight between a crocodile and a leopard; and thus treated, they produce much the same effect as a Roman mosaic.

In short, the habit of wearing shells as personal decoration is a very ancient one. But it persists today. I have a friend, for example, who owns a handsome necklace made up of shells that come, she assures me, not from the sea, but from the Falums of Touraine, deposits of the Miocene Age, rich in fossil marine shells. The extraordinary thing about them is their condition: many of them are so well preserved that they retain the glazed surface of living specimens.

21 William Dampier, author of *Observations on the Coast of New Holland*, 1699. Portrait by T. Murray

The Early Collectors and their Cabinets

JOHN TRADESCANT, who possessed the first recorded collection of 'natural curiosities', including many shells, to be publicly exhibited, was a strange and interesting character, as indeed were most of the early naturalists. There are several portraits of him in the Ashmolean Museum at Oxford, which show him to have been black-haired and bearded, with intelligent, staring eyes. The exact date of his birth is unknown, but in 1618 he made a voyage round the North Cape to Archangel, and after-wards wrote a curious narrative full of details regarding the plants of Russia. When we next hear of him, he had joined an expedition against the Algerine corsairs as a gentleman volunteer, and brought back an apricot tree from North Africa. In 1625, he informed a friend in Virginia that he was in the service of the Duke of Buckingham, 'and that it was the Duke's pleasure for him to deal with all the merchants from all places, but specially from Virginia, Bermuda, New Foundland, Guinea, the Amazon and the East Indies, for all manner of rare beasts, fowls and birds,

22 (*opposite*) Two large *Murex radix*, a plate from Küster's *Conchylien*

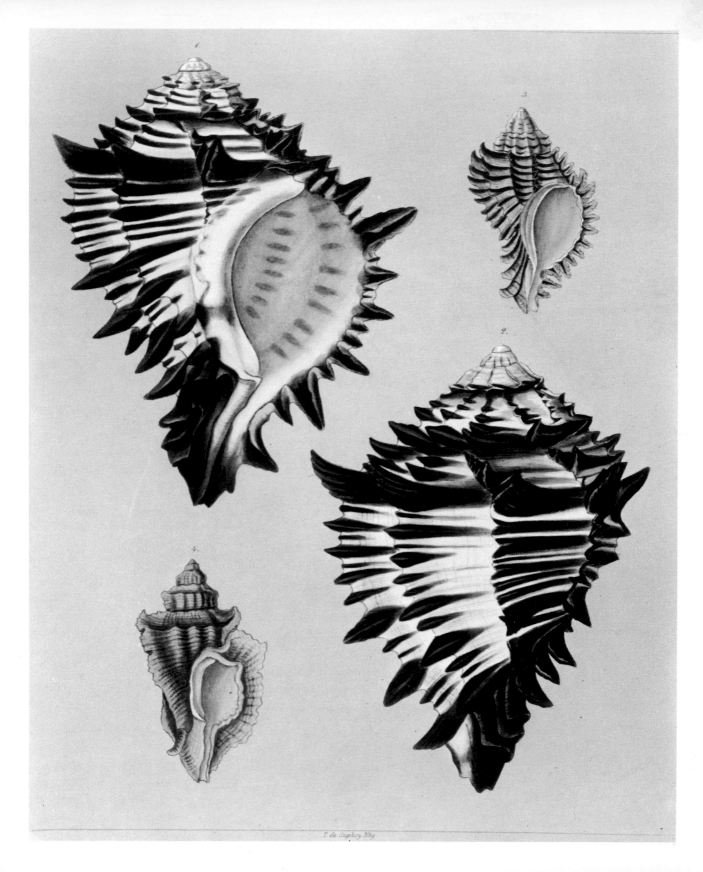

23 Elias Ashmole (1617-92), astrologer, alchemist and antiquarian. After J. Riley

24 An engraving by H. J. Redouté from the *Tableau Encyclopédique et Méthodique*, Paris, 1815

shells and stones'. This, undoubtedly, was when he picked up his own curious collection of miscellaneous objects with which his house in South Lambeth was filled. The house, called 'Tradescant's Ark', survived until 1881.

John Tradescant had a son whom he named after himself, and who inherited the 'Ark' and all its collections, including the 'physic' garden full of rare plants. John Tradescant Junior appears also to have inherited his father's bent for natural history; in 1657 he was off to the new colony of Virginia, gathering flowers, plants and shells for the collection at Lambeth. In 1656, Tradescant published his *Museum Tradescantianum*, 'a rare collection of rarities presented at South Lambeth near London'. He was assisted in the catalogue by Elias Ashmole, through whose hands the Tradescants' collection eventually passed, to become the Ashmolean Museum at Oxford. Various other friends made donations to the museum, men like William Courteen, whose collection of shells, when he died in 1702, was said by John Evelyn, the diarist, to be worth eight thousand pounds. The opening of the exhibition must have been a very grand affair, for it was attended by King Charles II and all the Court. The catalogue contained a list of birds, quadrupeds, fish, shells, insects, minerals, fruits, war-instruments, habits, utensils, coins and medals, followed by a list in English and Latin of the plants in the garden. 'The wonderful variety and incongruous juxtaposition of the objects', writes Sir William Flower in his *Essays on Museums*, 'made the catalogue very amusing reading. Among "whole birds" is the famous Dodar from the Island of Mauritius.' The head and foot of this stuffed Dodo is still preserved in the Oxford University Museum, together with the portrait of John Tradescant the younger, probably by Emanuel de Critz [figure 19]. Painted at about the time of the exhibition, it recalls his father's dark, foreign face and intent stare. With him is a friend, a Quaker brewer of Lambeth, masquerading under the fictitious name of Zythepsa, a suitably strange character with an enormous nose that gives him the appearance of a vegetable composition by Archimboldo. Piled up on a velvet-covered table on Tradescant's right is a collection of his most impressive shells, which one immediately recognizes: a beautiful specimen of the large *Charonia tritonis* or triton shell [figure 80], and next to it a member of the genus *Turbo*, the outer skin peeled off, exposing its nacreous lining; a cone shell, and behind it a large trochus. Topping the pyramid are the spidery claws of the East Indies' *Lambis rugosa* [figure 125]. Branches of coral and other shells round out the composition.

Among their contemporaries were some equally impassioned shell collectors. One was William Dampier, the buccaneer and navigator, who started life as an assistant-manager of a plantation in Jamaica [figure 21]. In his *Observations on the Coast of New Holland*, published in 1699, he mentions the shells he observed in Sharks Bay: 'The shore was lined thick with many other sorts of very strange and beautiful shells, a variety of colours and shapes, most freely spotted with red, black and yellow, etc, such I have not seen anywhere but this place.' Another was Sir Hans Sloane, whose collection was bequeathed to the nation, to become the nucleus of the material now housed in the British Museum of Natural History [figure 25]. In 1707 he published the first volume of his excellent natural history book, *A Voyage to the Islands of Madeira, Barbados, Nièves, St Christopher and Jamaica*, which he dedicated to Queen Anne. On the death of Sir Isaac Newton, in 1727, Sloane was elected President of the Royal Society where he held office until 1741. Meanwhile he had been steadily collecting; his natural taste seems to have been stimulated by John Tradescant's friend, William Courteen; and we know exactly to what extent it was stimulated, for he spent as much as fifty thousand pounds acquiring new and rare examples of shells. As Dezallier d'Argenville tells us in his book on shells, published in Paris in 1742, Sloane's was *le plus beau cabinet que j'ay vu en Angleterre. Il semble que les Indes se soient épuissées pour remplir tous ses tiroirs*'.

In 1749 Sloane made a will bequeathing his collection to the nation, on condition that twenty thousand pounds should be paid to his family; and in 1753, the year of his death, an Act of Parliament was passed accepting the gift and appointing trustees to manage the collection. The following year, to show off their new treasures to more advantage, the trustees purchased Montague House, re-naming it *Museum Britannicum*.

If one looks through the British Museum papers, it becomes obvious that many of the original shells in this collection dated from the mid-seventeenth century, and had personal associations with Courteen, Dampier, Sloane and other contemporary author-naturalists and travellers.

It was assumed, however, that, after the passage of over two hundred years, various moves and the acquisition of much new material, these shells could no longer be identified, if, indeed, they still existed. Everybody was astonished, when the collection was being reorganized, to find that at least four hundred of Sloane's original specimens could still be picked out [figure 27]. Shells do not age perceptibly, though they fade if they are exposed to the light; but, since these shells had been locked away in mahogany cabinets, there was no reason why they should decay. The late Guy Wilkins, a one-time officer in the British Museum, explains in a Museum publication how they were able to trace them; it was a question of calligraphy. The numbers penned in the interior of the shells corresponded exactly with those in the catalogue; and it is clear that the specimens were numbered as the entries were made, and by the same hand—satisfactorily proved to be that of Sloane himself.

More or less contemporary with Tradescant, and a little Sir Hans Sloane's senior, was Martin Lister, who with his *Historia Conchyliorum* produced the first practical, systematic work on conchology. The book contained over a thousand copper-plate engravings of shells. Nothing on this scale was again attempted until well on into the eighteenth century; and Lister's work still holds an important place in conchological literature. Sloane is known to have worked with Lister's book open in front of him, constantly identifying his specimens with the copper-plate engravings, usually giving the plate and figure numbers. When Wilkins discovered this, he checked the specimens again, and found 'that not only were they comparable with Lister's figures, but that in many instances they were the actual specimens from which the plates were engraved by the author's two daughters' [figure 27].

It would seem that the *Historia Conchyliorum* was entirely a family affair. Lister's two daughters, Susanna and Anna, engraved all the plates in copper from their own drawings or washes—a work, as Wilkins points out, 'that must have occupied rather more than their leisures for over seven years'. With careful study, one can recognize the two sisters' work by their different techniques; Anna had a strong direct method of graduated lines, and Susanna a light cross-hatch style.

This rapid review of England's early collectors will have given us a general idea as to the kind of people who

25 Sir Hans Sloane, whose shell-collection was bequeathed to the British nation. Portrait by Slaughter, 1736

were forming natural history cabinets during the latter part of the seventeenth and the beginning of the eighteenth centuries; but to get a picture of what the cabinets looked like we must cross the Channel and, in the company of Dezallier d'Argenville, the eighteenth-century French naturalist, visit some of the best known Dutch and French collections; for it was in these two countries that the finest cabinets were to be found. Holland probably had the most spectacular; in no other country did the mania

26 John Tradescant the younger, and his friend, Zythepsa of Lambeth. Portrait attributed to Emanuel de Critz

for acquiring shells reach such heights. But then, of course, no country had a better reserve to draw on than Holland, thanks to her rich East India trade and her island colonies. In England, as we have already seen, shell-collecting was practised by a fortunate few; in Holland, the collectors were people of many different kinds. The Dutch were addicted to periodic crazes; during the first quarter of

25

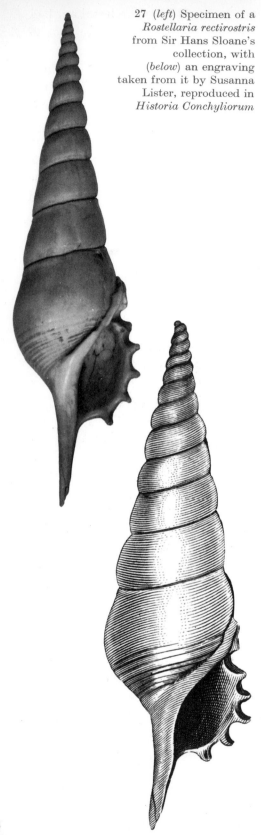

27 (left) Specimen of a
Rostellaria rectirostris
from Sir Hans Sloane's
collection, with
(below) an engraving
taken from it by Susanna
Lister, reproduced in
Historia Conchyliorum

the seventeenth century tulips had been imported from Constantinople; and everyone speculated on this new market. It is hardly surprising therefore that, when the Dutch East Indiamen began to arrive with exotic shells from tropical seas, a new market should suddenly have sprung up.

In those days the rare shells were the cones, cowries, mitres and volutes, with a few miscellaneous species belonging to other genera such as the thorny oyster, wentletrap, harp and *Rostellaria*. Many of the stories related about the extravagant prices paid for particular shells are probably apocryphal. We are told, however, that a botanist in Paris paid the equivalent of two hundred and forty pounds or six hundred and eighty dollars for a thorny oyster or *Spondylus regius* and that a duchess gave an estate for a wentletrap or *Scalaria pretiosa* or *Epitoneum scalare* as it is sometimes called [figures 88, 91]. The prices were indeed high; the left-handed *Turbinella pyrum* or sacred chank usually fetched about a hundred and seventy pounds or four hundred and seventy dollars [figure 115]. But these high sums do not necessarily indicate that the shell was scarce; what is rare in collection need not, by any means, be rare in nature [figure 28]. Fluctuating fashions had, and still have, a certain influence on prices; and we must also remember that the early naturalists seldom troubled to record the provenance of shells; with the result that some were in short supply for years until their place of origin had been rediscovered.

We now come to the cabinets themselves. In Holland, they were mostly situated around Amsterdam and the ports served by the Dutch East India Company; and, as Madame van Benthem Jutting, Curator of Molluscs at the Zoological Museum of Amsterdam, tells us, only a few of their owners had any real scientific interest, especially when they collected many other objects—shells, insects, birds, plants and miscellaneous curiosities. During the seventeenth and eighteenth centuries, the arrangement of cabinets of shells differed entirely from the nineteenth-century method. It was the custom to exhibit them as elegantly as possible, sometimes working the shells themselves into geometrical figures, or grotesques imitating human or animal forms. There was little attempt at scientific classification. Dezallier d'Argenville, the eighteenth-century French naturalist, describes them for us—a task, as he points out in his *La Conchyliologie ou Traité Général des Coquillages de Mer*,

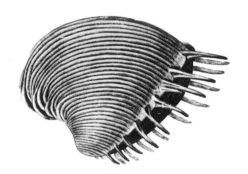

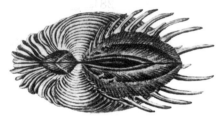

28 *Venus dione*, once considered so rare that Rumphius offered £1,000 for it. An engraving by H. J. Redouté from the *Tableau Encyclopédique et Méthodique*,

(Paris, 1780), that he never would have undertaken, had he himself not visited all the most famous cabinets of Europe.

His descriptions evoke long suites of rooms entirely lined with glass-fronted cupboards [figure 30]. The cupboards are beautifully finished and highly gilded; so are the many-drawered cabinets. The first section of one of these cabinets would be devoted to the vegetable world, and would contain different kinds of fruit, woods, roots, barks and leaves arranged in glass jars. Flowers would be dried and stuck into books. On coming to the second section, d'Argenville tells us, we should have had an agreeable surprise; it was given over to the animal kingdom, and contained all kinds of birds and strange creatures, stuffed and fixed with wire to the ceiling [figure 29]. He admits that it is not usual to see fish or quadrupeds in the air, but assures us that they look splendid and stand out well against the white plaster. Other cupboards on our tour would contain beaks and claws and jawbones of exotic animals, or lovely butterflies from Surinam, or jars of *eau-de-vie camphrée* in which floated human embryos, snakes, frogs, *et les souris et rats des Indes*. Finally, we should reach the shells ranged in large drawers. 'The cupboard in which they are kept is called a *coquillier*, the same way that one calls a cupboard one keeps medals in a *medaillier*.' The drawers, d'Argenville explains, should be lined with satin or velvet to prevent the shells from rolling. In Holland, he adds, they are lined with a crude linen; but he not does comment on the fact. Nowadays, of course, linen seems a far more suitable background.

The real naturalist, says d'Argenville, arranges his shells according to species and families, ignoring the question of size or symmetry, in this way mixing the handsome shells with the ordinary ones. The ordinary collector, on the other hand, had little interest in science, and the whole arrangement of his cabinet was governed by aesthetic considerations. He arranged his shells according to colour and texture, which, of course, was very pleasing to the eye.

Still in d'Argenville's company, we tour the other countries of Europe. In France, Louis XV was busily engaged adding to his gallery situated in Les Jardins des Plantes. The Duc de Bourbon had a very handsome cabinet at Chantilly with his shells arranged in drawers lined with green taffeta. Turgot, Governor of Guyenne, specialized in cones and petrified woods, and had over five thousand

27

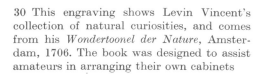

29 The Natural History Museum of the Emperor Ferdinand III of Germany. An engraving from *Historia Naturale di Ferrante Imperato*, Venice, 1672

30 This engraving shows Levin Vincent's collection of natural curiosities, and comes from his *Wondertoonel der Nature*, Amsterdam, 1706. The book was designed to assist amateurs in arranging their own cabinets

different kinds of sulphurs—all the different yellows possible. After the Court, it would seem that the clergy led the shell collecting world in France. The Benedictines of the Abbey of St Germain-des-Prés had the largest branch of white coral ever seen and, among other interesting things, a petrified bunch of grapes. d'Argenville also visited ladies in Dijon, Bordeaux, Reims and Dieppe, the last of whom specialized in spiny oysters; and at Le Havre he met a trader who had a large fossilized nautilus with crystallized cells.

The Elector of Saxony in Dresden had turned a considerable part of the Swinger palace into galleries, his

31 *Voluta nivosa*, from Australia. A plate from William Swainson's *Exotic Conchology*, London, 1821

32 *Nautilus pompilius*, from George Wolfgang Knorr's *Les Délices des Yeux et de l'Esprit*, Nuremberg, 1760

shells being arranged among what looked like branches of pine formed by crystals of silver from Peru. In Rome d'Argenville visited the Chigi and Barberini palaces; and he notes the existence of collections in Basle, Zürich, Lausanne and the Iberian Peninsula. Whichever author we consult it is always the Dutch cabinets that are the most admired; and in his *Catalogue Raisonné de Coquilles*, published in 1736, Gersaint informs us that the Dutch were also masters in the art of cleaning shells, and adds that they were more practised than anyone else for the simple reason that so many passed through their hands, coming from the East Indies.

The advice given is still valid today. We are reminded that many shells have an outer horny covering called an epidermis, which generally resembles a coat of varnish and serves probably to protect them. This one is advised to rub off with pumice stone, after having steeped the shell in a bowl of nitric acid. The mouth of the shell, where the nacre is exposed, should be covered with wax, so that the acid does not bite into it and damage the colour. The action of the acid will also form a kind of foam on the outer skin; and the shell should be withdrawn now and then and plunged into ordinary water, to make sure that it is not being damaged. If the shell happens to have a tapering spire or horn-like spurs, these, too, should be covered with wax. One is warned to wear thick gloves during this operation of steeping, in case one should yellow one's nails or even lose them.

One is also instructed as to how to brush up the shells—'hints', I may add, to be studiously ignored, such as smoothing off the shell with very fine sandpaper, and then brushing it with a thin varnish, or the white of egg, to make it shine. Later, this 'cleaning' of shells became a lucrative business. Shells were touched up in much the same way as a bad restorer overpaints a picture; corroded spots on the surface of the shell were rubbed off and chipped apertures filed smooth; scars and cracks were ingeniously hidden by fillings of wax. Merchants even went as far as to paint their shells unnatural colours. Certain species of murex, *Murex radix* for instance [figure 22], which by nature should be partially black, were sometimes too light to attract the eyes of the collector. The remedy was simple—they were treated with soot, which would be burnt into the shell over a lamp. One writer is particularly scathing about the habit of engraving

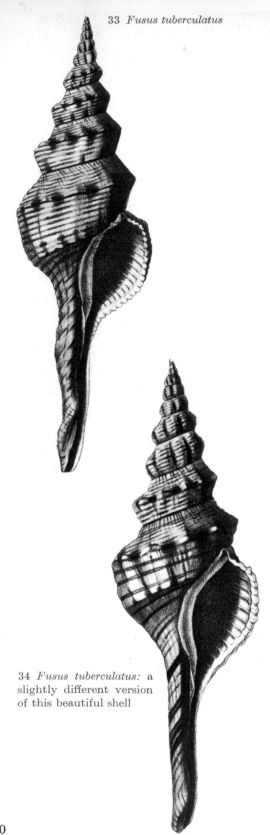

33 *Fusus tuberculatus*

34 *Fusus tuberculatus*: a slightly different version of this beautiful shell

and chiselling scenes on the nacreous surface of nautili and turbos, treatment that a great many of the mounted shells received [figure 35]. '*L'habitude de peindre les coquilles dont les Hollondais sont accusés, n'est nullement à suivre; c'est une supercherie qu'un naturaliste doit ignorer: plus il s'approche de la nature, plus l'art doit s'éloigner de lui.*'

But before we leave this world of creaking parquet floors and gilded cabinets, we must again cross the English Channel, to visit the Dowager Duchess of Portland's collection, which was probably the largest in Europe. The celebrated Linnaeus himself had seen it [figure 44]; and Dr Daniel Solander, the botanist who sailed with Joseph Banks on Cook's first voyage round the world, had at one time worked there. Banks was a frequent visitor to her great house at Bulstrode in Buckinghamshire; and there is little doubt that the pick of many novelties brought home by Byron, Wallace and Cook found their way to the crowded cabinets of Bulstrode or her London house in Whitehall. On her death, her collection was put up for auction. The sale, comprising over four thousand separate lots, opened on 24 April 1786, and continued for the next thirty-seven days, prices ranging from a few shillings for odd lots of shells and fossils to £ 1,029 for the famous Portland Vase, the *pièce de résistance* of the whole collection. The Rev. John Lightfoot, the Duchess's librarian and chaplain, compiled the catalogue, which makes instructive reading [figure 36]. On the first day, Lot No. 2 consisted of a partitioned box containing a great variety of small shells, sorted for making flowers, etc. This fetched nine shillings. Lot No. 13 brought the *Voluta melo*, or great African melon; another lot, No. 103, consisted of four-dozen-and-a-half leopard cowries.

The sale of the famous Portland collection raises a point of some interest. What became of most of these seventeenth and eighteenth-century cabinets? As we have already seen, some private collections eventually reached museums; but the greater part of them seem completely to have disappeared. Of this bygone glory, as Madame Jutting sadly remarks, all that remains 'are just the catalogues and a few pictures'. The pictures she refers to are the various still-lifes by artists such as Hoefnagel, Vosmaer and van der Ast, who used tropical shells as additional embellishments in their compositions of flowers and fruit. It is not a question of a few score of fragile specimens falling into decay, but of thousands of solid marine shells. Certainly,

35 (*above*) An excellent example of an engraved *Nautilus pompilius*, now supported on a silver stand but made to hang from the ceiling. Its original owner, an important official in the Dutch Admiralty, ordered it in 1660 from Cornelius Bellekin, one of the celebrated family of engravers. The figures are after drawings by Jacques Callot

they did not perish through lack of appreciation; for we have seen with what enthusiasm the collectors set to work. 'It is terrible', wrote a French conchologist in 1767, 'that such a splendid collection containing so many thousands of specimens should be dispersed in a few days by public sale. The collection has taken years to assemble; both Indies have contributed to it, and it has been enriched by the cabinets of half the world. Now in its turn this collection is to disappear, with the only result that other collections will fill their empty spaces from it, and they, too, will eventually suffer the same fate.'

36 Frontispiece to the *Catalogue of the Portland Museum*, 1786

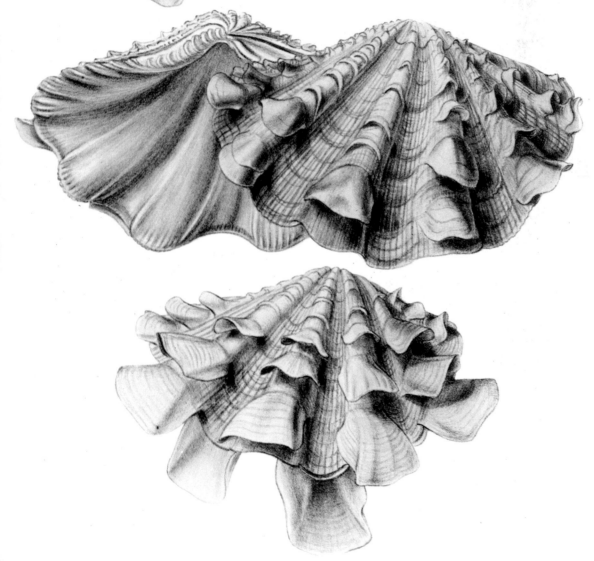

Handbooks
and
Nomenclature

37 The elaborately sculptured *Tridacna squamosa*, a plate from *Conchologia Iconica* by Lovell Reeve

38 Two views of a *Murex*: a plate from the *Index Testarum Conchyliorum* by Nicolai Gualtieri, Florence, 1742

THE PREVIOUS CHAPTER has given a glimpse of the collecting world in the seventeenth and eighteenth centuries; I now turn to the series of handsome reference books that early collectors were fortunate enough to have at their disposal. All these works included black-and-white engravings; while many of them were copiously illustrated with excellent coloured plates—plates as eagerly collected nowadays as the shells that they depict. Since the present book contains a few reproductions of plates selected from the best of such works, something must be said about their authors.

In English, as we have already seen, Lister was the pioneer; and after him came Thomas Martyn, Da Costa and Perry; the Dutch being represented by Rumphius, Valentijn, Seba and Gronovius, and the Italians by Gualtieri and Buonnani [figure 38]. Germany had Knorr, Born, Lesser and Klein; in Denmark we find Regenfuss, and in France d'Argenville and Bruguière. There were others, of course, but the writers listed above were the most popular.

In his *Délices des Yeux et de l'Esprit*, published in Nuremberg in 1760, George Wolfgang Knorr complains how hard it is to come by the works of his fellow naturalists. They were out of print, 'and one comes across them only by greatest chance'. That, he explained, is why he has embarked upon his own work—together with the fact that so little is known about 'the wonders of nature that lie close hidden in the very bosom of the Ocean itself'. 'Scientists of our age', he continues, 'are making every effort to perfect our knowledge in natural history. One sees proof of their indefatigable application in every branch of this science. Everything has been subject to their research, from the most insignificant grain of sand to the most splendid of diamonds; from the highest cedars of Lebanon to a clump of hyssop growing against the wall. However, there still remain a few things in the domain of natural history on which we lack information and these [he refers to shells] seem all the more difficult to procure since one only comes across them by chance. It is only a happy accident which brings us examples of these beautiful creations of nature.' Knorr's coloured plates, however, are on the whole very fine, particularly his magnificent representation of the *Nautilus pompilius*, engraved by himself after a painting by B. R. Dietschin [figure 32].

I have no space here to give an account of all the early

33

39 George Everhard Rumphius, engraved by T. de Later, 1650. It is interesting to note that Later clearly indicates the blindness which afflicted Rumphius in old age.

40 *Harpa ventricosa*, an engraving from Rumphius' *Amboinese Curiosity Cabinet*

41 *Babylonia spirata*

naturalists named; but an exception must be made for the Dutch botanist and conchologist, George Everhard Rumphius, who was far in advance of most contemporary naturalists [figure 39]. He was called the 'Pliny of the Indies'; and, being in the service of the Dutch East India Company, he was the first naturalist to observe his subjects in the field and keep an accurate record of the places where they were found—an important point in shell-collecting. Few eighteenth-century naturalists equalled the high standard of his *Amboinese Curiosity Cabinet*. Certainly his work stimulated collecting among the merchant adventurers of the time and no doubt helped to give Holland its leadership in the shell-collecting world. Rumphius also had an extraordinary talent for description and nomenclature, and his text was beautifully illustrated [figure 40]. The descriptions we owe to Rumphius alone; but for the illustrations he had the assistance of several artists, one of them being Pieter de Ruyter.

This seems an appropriate moment to deal with the problem of nomenclature; and here we must again refer to Madame van Benthem Jutting, for she is by far our best source of information concerning the early collections. She tells us that the names of shells used in books were sometimes scientific, sometimes vernacular, and that occasionally both are found side by side. The scientific names were in Latin; and very often the longest and most unpronounceable names were bestowed on minute and nearly microscopic species. Between 1737 and 1768 Carl von Linné, or Linnaeus, the famous Swedish naturalist, had written and published twelve editions of the *Systema Naturae* which revolutionized all biological nomenclature; but this only affected later works [figure 44]. 'For the vernacular names', writes Madame van Benthem Jutting, 'the designations of the early Dutch authors, Rumphius and Valentijn, were in current use. So great was the influence exercised by these pioneers that their nomenclature figured in many contemporary French and German treatises, either literally translated, or freely adapted.' Rumphius gave, in addition to normal scientific names, popular Dutch names to nearly all the shells he handled, many of which had been invented by the sailors. Some of these were ironical, and some, naturally enough, a trifle scabrous. Perry, the early nineteenth-century conchologist, points to the *Chama lazarus*, an imbricated and spinous bivalve, as an example of the Swedish naturalist's 'usual want of

42 An engraving of *Cypraea arabica* from Martin Lister's *Historia Conchyliorum*

43 A hand-painted plate representing a striped *Bulla*, from Thomas Martyn's *Universal Conchologist*, London, 1784-92

44 Carl von Linnaeus, the famous Swedish naturalist

delicacy' [figure 45]. 'He named it *lazarus* from its resemblance to an infected sore, a denomination certainly more ingenious than agreeable.' Madame Jutting bears out Perry in his suggestion that Linnaeus and 'contemporary and successive systematists' were not very delicate when it came to choosing names—no better in fact than the rough-and-ready sailors. The decent obscurity of the Latin language cannot disguise their fundamental meaning.

Despite their occasional indecency, it was the popular names that appealed to the cabinet owners; and it is still the popular names that many amateur collectors prefer to use today. The trouble with this system is that vernacular names will vary from language to language. The problem is further complicated because few of the early naturalists could agree regarding the division of the different species; and not until the end of the eighteenth century were shells being properly classified. Collectors were warned not to be too impressed by the brilliant colours of their shells, but to examine their extremities and convolutions, their whorls, whether ventricose or inflated, and a dozen other more scientific details. Such sound advice proved that there was a new spirit abroad. Indeed, the early days of the nineteenth century were to revolutionize the conchological world. Scientific expeditions were embarked on, both by naturalists and by collectors; and methods of arranging collections were also to undergo a change. 'Instead of table cases', writes Madame Jutting, 'and drawers with shell bouquets, mosaics and festoons, a more scientific fashion gained ground. The shells were arranged systematically and put into trays and boxes, or gummed on cards.'

The dawn of the nineteenth century not only saw improvements in the study of shells and in the way they were collected; it awoke a new sense of responsibility among the owners of cabinets. Now that many natural history museums were being founded, it was easy to find a proper resting-place for the collection after the collector's death. At the same time, conchological reference books improved in quantity and quality. As Wilkins writes, 'the opening of the Sloane collection to the public in 1759 under the new title of the British Museum and the engagement of the nucleus of a scientific staff, made a vast quantity of unknown material available to authorities of the late eighteenth and early nineteenth centuries. Writers and conchologists were not slow to grasp the opportunity

35

45 The *Chama lazarus*, so-called by Linnaeus for its resemblance to an infected sore. An engraving from the *Tableau Encyclopédique et Méthodique* by Lamarck, Paris, 1815

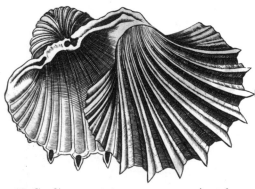

46 *Cardium costatum*, an engraving from Martin Lister's *Historia Conchyliorum*

and thus began an era of scientific and popular publication that reached its zenith with the production of Lovell Reeve's *Conchologia Iconica*'. Captain Cook's three voyages also made their mark on the period; for they opened up vast coastlines hitherto known only vaguely as the *Terra Australis Incognita*, from which plants and animals were brought back in almost too great a profusion to be dealt with by the few naturalists capable of the task. Between 1798 and 1822 Lamarck published in Paris his *Histoire des Animaux Sans Vertèbres* and contributed to the *Tableau Encyclopédique et Méthodique* [figure 47]; and, a few years later, Deshayes brought out his *Traité Elémentaire de Conchyliogie*; while Lamarck's pupil Duclos produced *Coquilles Univalves Marines* [figure 117]. These works ran to several volumes and took some years to complete. In Germany we have the *Conchilien Cabinet* by Martini and Chemnitz [figure 96]; and in England Perry's *Conchology* published in 1811 [figure 81]. Perry is very popular with bibliophiles, but due to his inaccuracies, he was, for long, treated with contempt by expert conchologists. Not so Martyn's *Universal Conchologist or Figures of Non-descript Shells Collected in the Different Voyages to the South Seas since the year 1764*, which compared with Perry is very thorough [figure 43]. Then, in the eighteen-twenties, we get Swainson's excellent *Exotic Conchology* [figure 31].

In his Introduction, Thomas Martyn points out proudly that he is the first natural history draughtsman to concentrate on depicting two views of each shell. He presumes that the method he has adopted 'of displaying the figure of each shell in two positions, would generally be preferred, giving a more perfect knowledge of the subject'. He tells us that 'the shells depicted have been collected by the several officers of the ships under the command of Captains Byron, Wallace, Cook and others, in the different voyages they made to the South Seas'.

Martyn complains that, in his day, none of the good artists would devote their talents to the task of drawing shells. 'Of the miniature painters who excel, it can never be worth their while without a very liberal compensation.' This decided him, 'at very great expense', to establish an Academy of Youths, for which he recruited boys who, 'born of good but humble parents, could not from their own means aspire to the cultivation of the liberal arts'. Naturally, these youths were expected to possess a natural gift for drawing and painting, and worked under his im-

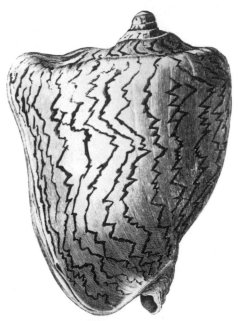

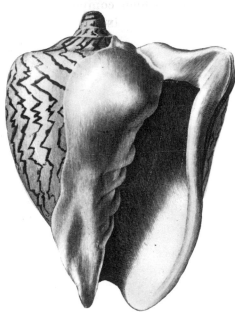

47 *Voluta scapha*, engraving from the *Tableau Encyclopédique et Méthodique*

mediate inspection and control. The experiment succeeded; and he had ten apprentices working for him on his *Universal Conchologist*. In a little over three years, he managed to produce seventy copies of the first two volumes of this work. The plates were all hand-painted, which involved the production of about six thousand duplicate paintings of shells. Some, but not all of the plates, are excellent; and, for his own and his pupils' pains, he was awarded gold medals by Pope Pius VI, the Emperor Joseph II of Austria, Ferdinand IV of Naples and Charles IV of Spain [figure 43].

Martyn's *Universal Conchologist* is an impressive work; but of a far superior quality are William Swainson's plates in his *Exotic Conchology*, published in 1821. They are certainly among the most beautiful coloured plates that exist; the shells seem to have alighted on the paper, and been brushed into place with gossamer tracings. The delicacy of touch is extraordinary [figure 31].

Good as some of these works were, the books published towards the middle of the nineteenth century were even better. Lovell Reeve's *Conchologia Iconica* [figure 116] and Sowerby's *Thesaurus Conchyliorum* [figure 49] appeared at a time when the demand for fine hand-coloured engravings, as guides to the identification of shells, was at its height. During the heyday of the Victorian era, shell-collecting became a popular hobby. By building the Brighton Pavilion the Prince Regent had already set the seal of fashion on the habit of taking seaside holidays; but now many other towns in Great Britain and the United States were beginning to follow Brighton's example, and millions of middle-class citizens now swarmed every summer into the new seaside towns. Shell-collecting, once the prerogative of a few naturalists and gentlemen of leisure with a taste for the exotic, became the pastime of every small child.

Meanwhile eminent naturalists continued to study seashore life from a more scientific point of view and write treatises on the plants and animals of the zone between the tides. Several important scientific voyages were sponsored by official bodies; one of them took Charles Darwin on the voyage of the *Beagle*, and another was carried out by Wyville Thomson on board the *Challenger*. Thomson was the first scientist to examine the possibilities of deep-sea dredging seriously, an innovation that was to change completely the whole course of shell-collecting. Certain shells that until then had been regarded as comparatively rare, now became almost common, with the result that today few specimens can be accounted scarce.

Univalves and Bivalves

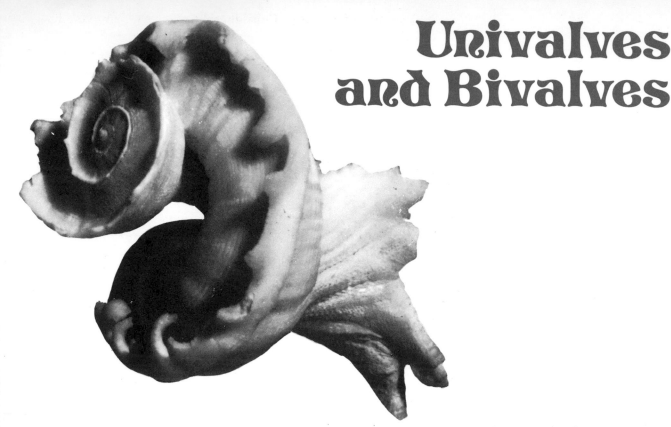

48 *Latiaxis mawae*

A LARGE SHELL sits in front of me on my desk. I know it of old, a triton that had belonged to one of my great-uncles. Were I to pick it up as I have so often done in the past, I should hear a loud humming like the unsleeping murmur of some distant surf—and suddenly as I write this, some lines of Charles Webb's come back to me:

> I sent thee a shell from the Ocean beach;
> But listen thou well, for my shell hath speech,
> Hold to thine ear and plain thou'll hear.

But what would I hear? The tales of Yankee whalers? Tales of the sailor lad my uncle used to be, or then perhaps tales of the shells themselves, for they certainly have fascinating stories to tell; the paper nautilus that Pliny describes as sailing across the waves, or then the *murex* from Tyre and Sidon from which the ancients extracted the purple to dye the robes of Imperial Rome.

But we must try to enlarge on the true character of a shell, or mollusc as it is more correctly termed. Formerly very little was known about the animal which formed and inhabited shells. The shell, or covering of the animal, alone attracted the attention of the student, hence the reason why this branch of natural science received the name of conchology. Considerable research, however, has been undertaken on the subject since then, and here, in the next few pages, I will try to note down the facts as simply as possible.

Broadly speaking, the molluscs are a large group of more than sixty thousand species and are, next to the insects, the largest assemblage of animals in existence. It was the great Cuvier, France's foremost naturalist, who, when seeking a name to include the entire class, and wishing to indicate the soft, boneless character of their bodies, selected the word 'mollusca' derived from the Latin *mollis*, soft. The group, or more correctly the *phylum* molluscs, is divided into four main orders, but only three really concern us here: the *Pelecypoda* or bivalves; the *Gasteropoda* or univalves; and the *Cephalopoda*, which includes the octopus and cuttle-fish. The two orders which interest us particularly are the bivalves whose shells are composed of two coverings, or plates, united by a hinge, and the univalves, or *Gasteropoda*, which are covered, as the name suggests, with a single spiral shell, like the ordinary land snail. The latter are the more extensive of the two orders.

The univalves, or gasteropods, have a distinct head and usually tentacles or horns with eyes at their tips and a foot or muscular disc on which they crawl about like a snail. Bivalves have no heads as a distinct part of their bodies, they are not deficient, however, in those organs of outer sense which characterize other molluscs. Many of them have numerous eyes for seeing, ears for hearing, filaments for touching, lips for tasting and mouths for taking their food. Many bivalves fertilize themselves, while univalves often have distinct sexes.

How does one describe the formation of the outer coating or shell of a mollusc? It is not easy. The shell may be regarded as a hardened or calcified case, specially provided—like the enclosing ribs of the vertebrae which afford protection to the breathing organs and heart—to protect the soft part of the animal from injury and the animal itself from the attacks of enemies. This shell is formed by the mantle or kind of outer skin. A slimy juice consisting of membranaceous tissue is consolidated by an admixture of carbonate of lime, exuded from the glands of this important organ and thickening in successive layers, becoming hardened and moulded on the body; at first simple and unadorned, it is later embellished according to the taste or inclination of the occupant. One

49 (*opposite*) The extraordinarily formed *Architectonica perspectiva*. The specimens figured are mostly from Hugh Cuming's collection. A plate from G. B. Sowerby's *Thesaurus Conchyliorum*, London, 1847

can be precise on this point but here investigation ends, since not even the microscope can help us when confronted with the creative power of nature. One is at a complete loss to understand the intricacies of structure and the varying shades of colour displayed by different molluscs. From the most rude and misshapen oyster, scarcely to be distinguished from its native rock, the scale regularly ascends till it arrives at perfection in the symmetry of

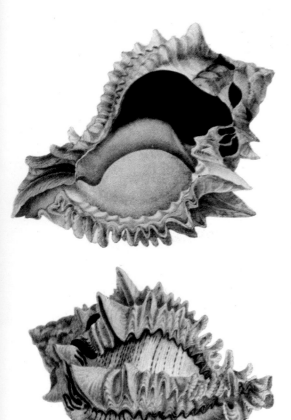

50 (*above*) *Murex Regius*, a plate in William Swainson's *Exotic Conchology*, London, 1821

51 (*right*) A plate from the Austrian edition of *La Conchologie ou Traité Général des Coquillages de Mer* by Dezallier d'Argenville, Vienna, 1772. The top shell represents *Murex tenuispina*, or Venus' comb

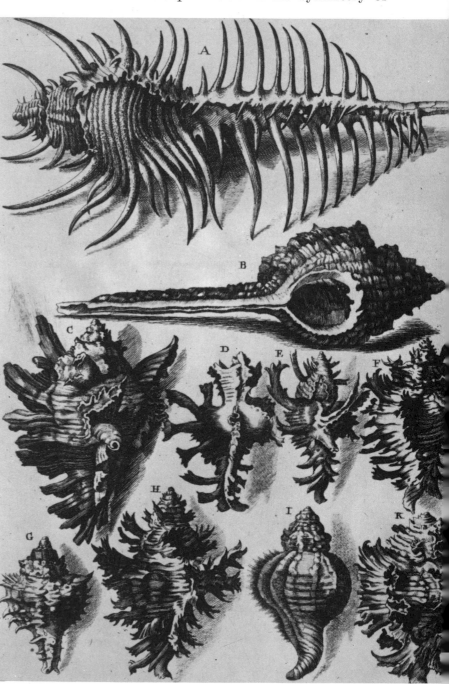

52 The elegant *Turritella terebra*

the spiral snail, the *Terebra subulata*, for instance, whose convolutions commencing in a point, and winding with an easy flow, insensibly dilate as they proceed, till the whole assumes the elegant taper of a cone [figure 122]. And how can one explain the architectural intricacy of the *Architectonica perspectiva* [figure 49], or the little spikes and spines of the *Murex tenuispina*, so poetically named in the vernacular as Venus' Comb [figure 56]. Cold facts tell us that the shell's mantle contains minute pores replete with colouring fluid, which blend invisibly with the calcareous exudation. But this does not explain the extraordinary patterns, shapes and colours, the horny explosions which some of the molluscs assume. Take, for example, the brilliant orange *Spondylus* from tropical waters, or the *Voluta musica* from the West Indies, with its notes of music clearly visible running round the shell [figure 104]. The beauty of the markings can hardly be explained away by the animal's need for camouflage. Edward Step, a Victorian naturalist, points out that the character of the shell is modified by the habits of the creature that makes it. 'This diversity of form is, no doubt, determined by the habit of the mollusc and the situation it inhabits. For example, those species that adhere to rocks in shallow water (such as the ordinary limpet) and are therefore subjected to the heavy beating of breakers, have their shells broad, smooth, and free from sculpturing that might catch the water and so result in the mollusc being swept away from its hold. Closely related species that live on sandy or gravelly bottoms appear, in many cases, to find the advantages in angles and knobs; probably because their foothold being precarious, when they are detached by waves, their irregular surface prevents them from being swept from the spot.'

The eyes of molluscs are somewhat rudimentary in their structure, and at times are little better than organs of touch. The highest development of the molluscan eye is found among the cuttle-fishes and their allies, but a pair of well-developed eyes is the possession of nearly all the molluscs that are furnished with heads, that is to say gasteropods. Yet the presence of a head is not absolutely essential for the acquirement of eyes. The coloured bulbs which fringe the mantle of a scallop are eyes, though it must be regarded as tolerably certain that these eye-substitutes are merely sensitive to light and are useless for observation.

53 *Trophon Catalinensis* from California

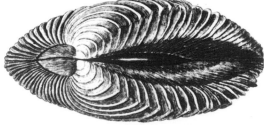

54 An engraving by H. J. Redouté from the *Tableau Encyclopédique et Méthodique*, Paris, 1815

Probably the most important of the senses to molluscs is that of smell. It is known to reach much farther than either vision or hearing. Great numbers of carnivorous molluscs, such as the common whelk, are found in lobster-pots, baited with 'high' fish. Whelks are largely used as bait, but are also eaten with relish by some people and fishermen have been known to procure them by placing a dead animal on the sand at low-water mark. John Gwyn Jeffreys describes it thus in *British Conchology*, 1863: 'The bait is completely covered with stones, which are piled up like a cairn, partly to prevent the carcass from being carried away by the tide, and also because fishermen have a scruple about eating shell-fish which have been fed on such carrion. On the next turn of the tide the heap of stones is visited and the whelks are found on the surface in great numbers, having been apparently attracted by the smell of the bait.'

The food of molluscs is very varied, as is their method of obtaining it. Some are carnivorous and cannibalistic, others are exclusively vegetarian, browsing on their pastures of sea-weeds like any herbivorous quadruped. Others feed entirely upon minute floating organisms caught up in the currents of water passing through their inhalant siphons. By far the greatest part of the molluscs are animal-eaters. The *Conidae*, for instance, all live predatory lives. The harps are carnivorous, so also are the *Buccinum* and the *Natica*. These latter have strong teeth for boring into shells and a long proboscis-like mouth and siphon, so that when burrowing after living bivalves on which they feed, they can protrude their mouths into their gaping valves, or drill holes even into the shell itself. If one looks carefully at the empty shells picked up on a beach, one finds that at least fifty per cent of them have a neat round hole drilled somewhere in the surface of their shell, a sure indication that they have been the subject of a succulent meal.

We have already explained how all univalves or gasteropods use the underside of their body, a form of muscular foot to creep or glide around on. The bivalves are far less mobile, although they all begin their lives in a free-swimming condition. Many of them, such as the oyster, move around for a week or two, then settle down, lose their power of locomotion and never again alter their position; most of them, however, have a tongue-shaped organ of progression which is muscular and extremely

43

55 *(left)* The once much-prized
Conus cedo-nulli

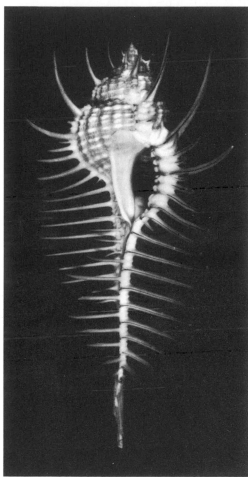

56 *Murex tenuispina*

57 *(right)* The rare *Conus gloria-maris*. There
are only twenty-five known specimens of this
shell in the world. This specimen is in the
Broderip collection, British Museum

flexible. Thrusting this foot through their half-open shells, they urge themselves along, ploughing through the sand with a succession of strong stabs. The foot of the cockle, for instance, enables it to leap to great heights, while in other cases it allows the creature to delve deep down into the sand. Apart from the nautilus, the only two molluscs that can actually swim are both bivalves: one is the scallop, or *Pecten,* and the other the *Lima.* They swim along in the water with most wonderful quickness, opening and flapping their valves together as they go. Their progress, however, is jerky and somewhat irregular, being traced in a series of zigzags. While on the shore they can move backwards and forwards by using the valves of their shell in a similar manner.

The difficulty of assigning special species of molluscs to particular zones is somewhat complex, temperature determining distribution. The greatest depth from which a mollusc has been taken so far is over three thousand fathoms. Large shells appear to be rare in the great ocean depths and are usually very fragile; even moderately sized specimens are far from common. The colour in the shells of deep-sea molluscs is never very pronounced and is often absent altogether. Fragile and wan, they hardly have the strength, at this great depth, to fend for themselves and feed on the 'rain' of dead animal matter which falls on the ocean floor, not so much hunting their prey as opening their mouths and eating whatever happens to come their way.

Among individual shells, the first to merit examination is the paper nautilus, the *Primos* of Aristotle, mentioned by him when describing the results of a scientific voyage which he was deputed to undertake during the reign of Alexander the Great. This puts us about three hundred and fifty years before the Christian era and one must suppose that it is the first fairly accurately described shell in history. The term nautilus simply means 'the sailor', its scientific name being *Argonauta argo,* again from the Greek, *Argo* having been the name of Jason's ship [figure 58]. It belongs to the *Cephalopoda* family and, along with the *Nautilus pompilius,* is the only member of the octopus family that secretes an external shell. This delicate white shell which Knorr charmingly describes as being so thin and light that one is not even conscious of having it in one's hand, is a distant cousin of the monster kraken. The kraken, or giant squid, was long considered

58 *Argonauta argo*

46

a monster of fable, but one day not so long ago, it suddenly became a reality when one was washed up at Placenta Bay, in Newfoundland. Its tapering body measured twenty feet, and its staring cruel eyes were as large as dinner plates and luminous at night like those of a cat. The strength of these giant *Cephalopoda*, with their long tentacular arms covered with sharp toothed suckers is almost incredible, and cases have been reported of titanic battles waged between them and enormous sperm whales. A life-sized model of such a combat can be seen in New York's Natural History Museum.

But this is not the correct atmosphere to evoke for our fragile paper-thin argonaut, the favourite of poets and artists of all ages. Aristotle describes it as floating on the surface of the sea in fine weather, holding out its sail-shaped arms to the breeze [figure 59]. Pliny endorses Aristotle's notion of its webbed arms spread out as a sail adding that its other arms, six in number, extended over the sides of its vessel, to act as oars. This legend regarding the paper nautilus's sailing propensity was very persistent and it is to be expected that poets would not fail to celebrate its nautical powers. Byron did so, and James Montgomery in his *Pelican Island* gives such an enchanting picture that even the naturalist can scarcely bring himself to wish that it was different:

> Light as a flake upon the wind,
> Keel upwards from the deep emerged a shell,
> Shaped like the moon ere half her horn is filled;
> Fraught with young life, it righted as it rose,
> And moved at will along the yielding water.

Of course the account so universally accredited is altogether fabulous. The nautilus, although sometimes floating on the surface, never moves in the manner described.

The *Argonauta* shell, in fact, is not a shell at all, but in reality the protective egg case of a female argonaut. The diminutive male of the species, having no responsibilities in the caring for the eggs, is incapable of building a cradle and moves about naked throughout his life. The true function of the membranous discs on one pair of the animal's arms, those thought to have been the sails, is that of forming the shell, which it does by the secretion of a fibrous matter that dries to the texture of prismatic paper [figure 59]. They also act as anchors to the shell, for the animal has no form of attachment other than these

59 An engraving of the *Argonauta argo*, or paper nautilus, in its fabled position, from Cassell's *Natural History*, London, 1881

47

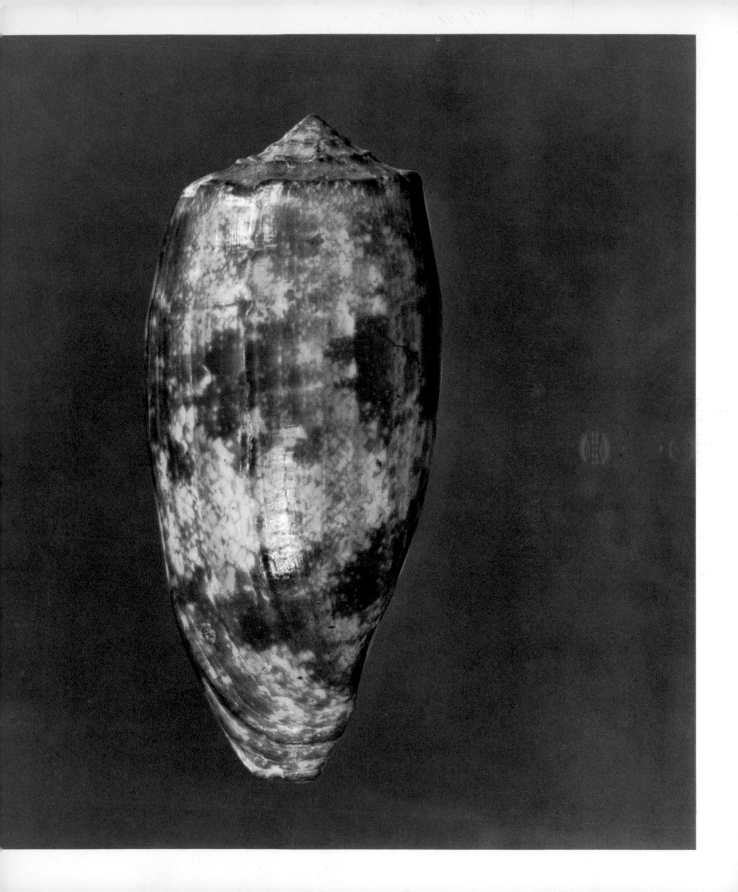

60 (*left*) The poisonous *Conus geographus*. This actual specimen, from the British Museum collection, is known to have killed a man

61 A fine specimen of *Cypraea aurantium* from the Fiji Islands

mantles with which she clasps it to her body. Several species of Argonauta are known and these are distributed for the most part in temperate zones. It is an inhabitant of the open sea and lives near the surface of the ocean. It moves swiftly, swimming backwards, by ejecting water from its funnel, like other cuttle-fish. The means by which it reproduces itself is interesting. One of the arms of the male is modified to form a sexual organ which

becomes detached and is deposited in the mantle cavity of the female during mating. The shell-less male, surprisingly enough, rarely exceeds an inch in length.

Another member of the nautilus family, the pearly nautilus, is so called from its superficial similarity to the original nautilus known to the Greeks. When compared with its relative, however, this shell has a very limited lineage, having been discovered in the fifteenth century by the Portuguese when they opened up the East Indies. The pearly nautilus is a native of tropical waters, inhabiting a restricted area between the Fiji Islands and the Philippines. It was Linnaeus who, in order to distinguish the two animals, took the name nautilus from the animal to which it originally belonged and bestowed it upon the very different East Indian mollusc, giving to the original nautilus the new name of *Argonauta*.

The resemblance of the *Nautilus pompilius* [figure 32] to the *Argonauta argo* [figure 58] is purely superficial; they can be compared only in that they are both inhabited by the same kind of animal, having arms or tentacles. The form and texture of the shells is quite different, the nautilus being heavy and porcelainous and striped a reddish brown over a pale beige ground, a combination of colours that made English sailors, when they first saw it floating on the water, exclaim that they had just met a drowned tortoiseshell cat. The inner part of the shell is nacreous and when scraped of its outer coating reveals the most brilliant sheen, turning from softest apple blossom to turquoise blue shot with green fire.

The shell consists of a series of chambers, the last formed of which is occupied by the body of the animal, the hinder ones, successively deserted, becoming air chambers, containing, in the healthy living animal, gas which serves to lessen the specific gravity of the whole organism. Among gasteropods it is not unusual to find the animal slipping forward in its shell as growth advances, thus leaving an unoccupied chamber in the apex of the shell. This may become shut off from the occupied cavity by a transverse septum, and a series of such septa may be formed, but only in the nautilus are these chambers known to contain gas [figure 63]. A further peculiarity of the nautilus shell is that the series of deserted air chambers are traversed by a cord-like pedicle extending from the soft part of the animal to the smallest and first formed chamber of the series. This membranous tube is known

62 *Anqaria imperialis*

as the *siphuncle* and constitutes the only attachment the animal has to its shell.

The *Nautilus pompilius* is mostly an inhabitant of deep water, being found àt two to three hundred fathoms. The animal remains mostly at the bottom, creeping sometimes into hoopnets set for fish or lobster-pots. It is undoubtedly a mistake to suppose that it ever comes to the surface voluntarily to swim about and is probably only washed up by storms, when injured by waves. Most living specimens obtained at different times by naturalists invariably appear to have been partly crippled and unable to dive again, no doubt because they had been brought up too suddenly from great depths. The animal is rarely seen, in fact, in the living condition. The empty shells, however, are often found washed up on the beach, but nearly always damaged. Rumphius during his long residence at Amboyna made a study of the nautilus and as usual has a considerable amount of interesting material on the subject. He tells us that empty shells are frequently to be found floating or cast up on the shore, 'for the defenceless animals, having no *operculum* (plate or horn of shell which many gasteropods have attached to their foot, serving to close the shell when the animal is retracted), are a prey to crabs and sharks who feed on them. Therefore', he explains, 'the shells are mostly found with the edges bitten off. Since the animal does not adhere fast to its shell, its enemies can easily drag it out, leaving the empty shell to float.' The young of this nautilus, he informs us, 'is not larger than a Dutch shilling and of a clear mother-of-pearl colour within and without'. According to Rumphius, they lose their rough outer coating due to the solvent action of the gastric juices to be found in a dolphin's stomach, 'from which most, if not all the young shells, of the pearly nautilus are usually obtained by collectors'.

How often has one come across the phrase 'born to the purple'; one thinks of the Byzantine emperors and particularly of Constantine VII who bore it among his personal titles. It either refers to the purple robes in which the imperial children were wrapped at birth, or to a chamber in the imperial palace called the *Porphyra* where the birth took place. Whether this *Porphyra* signified a chamber with purple hangings, or a room lined with porphyry, is not known. We have all heard, however, of the famous purple dye of Tyre and Sidon. As Browning writes:

63 A section of the *Nautilus pompilius*, showing the interior chambers traversed by a cord-like pedicle
Original gouache on vellum by P. Brown, about 1770

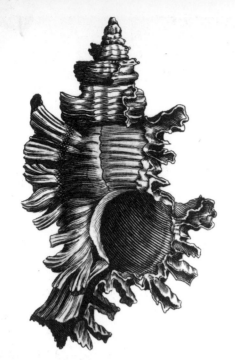

64 *Murex ramosus*, an engraving from Martin Lister's *Historia Conchyliorum*

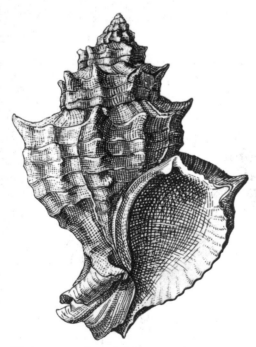

65 An engraving of *Murex trunculus*, from which the Tyrian purple dye was obtained by the ancients. From Moázzo's *Histoire de la Pourpre*, published in Alexandria in Greek

66 (*opposite*) Good examples of the small *Cypraea moneta*, or Money cowries

Who hath not heard how Tyrian shells
Enclose the blue, that dye of dyes,
Whereof one drop worked miracles,
And coloured like Astarte's eyes,
Raw silk the merchant sells?

Browning was wrong about the silk, for it was very fine wool that the emperors used in their togas. In the time of Augustus, one pound of this wool dyed with the Tyrian purple would cost about forty pounds or a hundred and ten dollars, and Pliny complains how every hour of use wears away robes of scarlet and purple which were almost as costly as pearls. But he must be forgiven his parsimony, for it is from him that we obtain most of our knowledge regarding the celebrated Tyrian purple of the ancients. He tells us how the dye was processed, explaining that is was obtained from a certain species of *murex* called *purpura*, a shell known to us as the *Murex trunculus*, an undistinguished-looking mollusc about an inch and a half long and of a drab brown colour, the ugly duckling of an otherwise particularly handsome family [figure 65]. Like many gasteropods it is carnivorous and used to be caught by the Tyrians in finely plaited lobster-pots baited with cockles [figure 68]. The dye was very costly owing to the small quantities which could be procured from each shell and to the many processes used in the dying. The material once stained, however, the colour was permanent, for Plutarch relates that the Greeks found a large quantity of purple cloth in the Royal treasury of Persia which was still rich and beautiful after having lain there for nearly two hundred years.

Pliny tells us that the small shells were bruised in a mortar and that the animals of the larger shells were taken out by hand. Following this, came a lengthy boiling process over a gentle fire, the workmen skimming off the fleshy impurities as they floated up to the surface. The boiling lasted ten days, then the dye was tested and if the colour produced proved defective, the boiling was renewed. To the ancients the colour known to us as purple comprises a variety of tints, including crimson and scarlet and much paler shades of these hues, the most popular being the rich crimson which Pliny likens to deep-red roses, or to congealed blood. These paler shades, he informs us, were obtained by diluting the dye with an equal quantity of human urine. Pliny's information is undoubtedly accurate, for heaps of crushed shells and

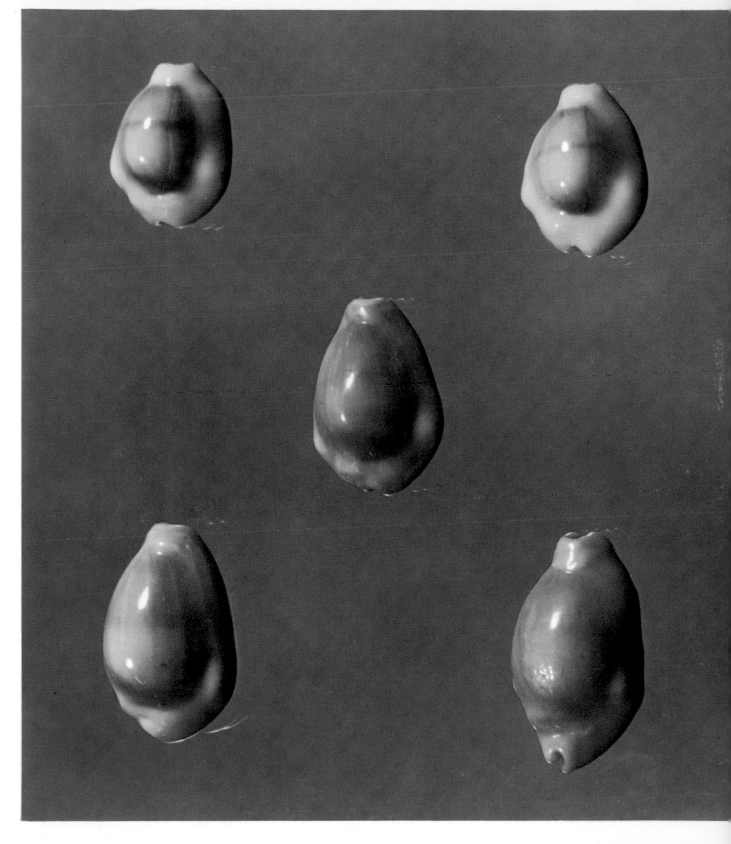

cauldron-shaped hollows are still to be found on Tyre's rocky shores.

We find that a similar dye was used in England at a very early period. The Venerable Bede, who wrote in the eighth century, mentions the art as a thing known in his days. The shell used, however, was not the *Murex trunculus* of the Mediterranean, but the common little 'purple' or dog periwinkle, as the *Nucella lapillus* is sometimes called. The colour was much lighter than that obtained from the *Murex trunculus* and it was used mainly for staining parchments or vellum with the idea of setting off the gold and silver lettering with which they were adorned. It would appear that the art was familiarly known and followed, but from its limited utility, and perhaps still more from its expense, it seems gradually to have gone into disuse, until at length only a few families preserved the knowledge of it, handing it down as a family secret. It was still being used in Ireland in 1684 for dyeing fine linen, but this seems to be its last public appearance.

So far, we have dealt with three specific shells chosen for their association with history. We now pass on to a specific family, the *Conidae*. Next to the *Cypraeidae* or cowries, they are the most beautiful group of gasteropod molluscs in the sea, also amongst the most numerous. Nearly three hundred living species have been described, but we shall deal with only a few of the better known ones here, the specially favoured *Conus cedo-nulli*, the famous *Conus gloria-maris*, the rare *Conus clytospira* and the various poisonous cones.

The family of cones is characterized by the remarkably persistent form of their shells, an inverted cone, with a very long and narrow aperture and a sharp-edged outer lip. They are solid and very heavy for their size, the largest measuring about six inches in length. The spire, in most cases, takes on the form of a flattened disc, each whorl falling so closely over its predecessor that the spiral nature of the shell is not perceived until it is viewed at right-angles to the spire. The *gloria-maris* [figure 57] and the *clytospira* [figure 74] are the main exceptions, both having elegantly marked spires, especially in the case of the *clytospira*. All the cones are porcelainous in their make-up, but in their living state are covered over with a yellowish brown epidermis or *periostracum*. This protective coating is thick and fibrous and very persistent and needs to be removed with considerable care. This accomplished,

67 Various cones from the *Tableau Encyclopédique et Méthodique*

ΑΠΟ ΜΙΑ ΣΑΡ
ΚΟΦΑΓΟ ΤΗΣ
ΣΙΔΩΝΟΣ ⲙ̄
"ΑΠΟ ΘΑΡ
ΣΙΣ ΗΞΕΙ
ΧΡΥΣΙΟΝ
ΜΩΦΑΖ ΚΑΙ
ΧΕΙΡ ΧΡΥΣΟ
ΧΟΩΝ ΕΡΓΑ
ΤΕΧΝΙΤΩΝ
ΠΑΝΤΑ ΥΑ·
ΚΙΝΘΟΝ ΚΑΙ
ΠΟΡΦΥΡΑΝ
ΕΝΔΥΣΩΣΙΝ
ΑΥΤΑ ⲟⲟⲓⲤΡΕΜΙΑΣ Χ.9

68 Bas-relief of a Tyrian fishing-vessel occupied in gathering shells for the manufacture of the famous purple dye

however, one is immediately struck by the diversity of pattern and colour which many of the specimens display.

Cones are found in southern and tropical seas, ranging northwards as far as the Mediterranean and southwards to the Cape of Good Hope. They become more numerous and more varied in their colours, however, as we approach the equatorial seas. Most cones inhabit deep waters, hiding in the holes and fissures to be found in submerged coral reefs. They are all cannibal and lead a predatory life, boring into the shells of other molluscs.

The species of cones so aptly named *cedo-nulli* were highly prized amongst the eighteenth-century collectors, and the colour-plate shown in this book explains the reason [figure 55]. The patterns splashed round the pleasing regularity of their forms are quite remarkable. *Cedo-nulli* was also considered to be extremely rare; indeed Knorr, writing in 1756, refers to it as unique. The specimen he illustrates is drawn with infinite care and was taken from a painting of the original then in the famous cabinet of Mr Lyonet at The Hague.

The prices paid for *cedo-nulli*, or *Koning von Zuidland* as the Dutch call it, were very high. One hears of it fetching three hundred and fifteen pounds as late as 1819, and then, as with most shells, the price dropped as soon as the exact location in which it occurred was rediscovered. Today, a good specimen would fetch about ten pounds or nearly thirty dollars, although *cedo-nulli* has always remained a favourite among collectors on account of the variety of paintings or markings that it exhibits.

Towards the end of the eighteenth century a new fancy popped up—the *Conus gloria-maris*, or the 'glory of the sea'. It is still considered the show-piece of any collection which is fortunate enough to possess it, and a dealer in London told me that he had a standing offer of a thousand dollars from a client in America should one ever turn up on the market. Although not by any means the rarest of all shells, it is still scarce enough to excite general interest among conchologists. Mr S. P. Dance of the Mollusca Section in London's Natural History Museum, who has made a special study of this shell, tells me that there are only about twenty-five specimens known. He considers that the adulation accorded to *gloria-maris* may be due, in part, to its name. Any shell known as 'the glory of the sea' is bound to attract attention. 'Collectors are hypnotised by it', he says. 'They are agog with excitement even before I unlock the cabinet. Usually they ask to touch a specimen and they often do so with trembling hands for fear they may break it.' Mr Dance also told me that *gloria-maris* is closely guarded these days, as one was stolen from a show-case in an American museum recently.

As can be expected, there are a great many stories regarding this rare cone. It is sometimes said that it is now extinct. Originally its only known locality was a small reef in the Philippine Islands, where in 1837, Hugh Cuming, the English conchologist, found three shells under a single rock. 'I fainted with delight', he said. A short time afterwards the reef was supposedly destroyed by an earthquake and with it, presumably, *gloria-maris*. It is a charming story, but completely inaccurate, for as recently as October 1957 another specimen was found, again in the Philippines, but not in the vicinity of the destroyed reef. After a typhoon, a young boy wandering about Corregidor Island, at the entrance to Manila Bay, found a very fine specimen.

In 1887 there were twelve known specimens of *gloria-maris* and only two during the early part of the previous century. In the circumstances there might be some truth in the story of the Frenchman who is related to have

69 *Latiaxis mawae*

possessed the only specimen except one which belonged to Hwass, the great Dutch collector. When this came under the hammer, he outbid every rival, and finally, taking possession of his treasure, is said to have thrown it on to the floor where he ground it to bits under his heel. 'Now', he exclaimed, 'my specimen *is* the only one.' Whether true or not he certainly did not eradicate *gloria-*

70 Three variously coloured *Strombus gallus* from Barbados

maris quite so easily, for it is far too solid a shell to treat in so off-handed a manner.

So notorious was the shell that it became the subject of a novel by Miss Fanny Steele, a Victorian lady who called her book *The Glory of the Sea* and set it in the village of Highcliff. The plot centred round the supposed theft of *gloria-maris*. Miss Crabbe, an eccentric old woman with a

57

71 These cones live in deep water, hiding in the holes of submerged coral reefs

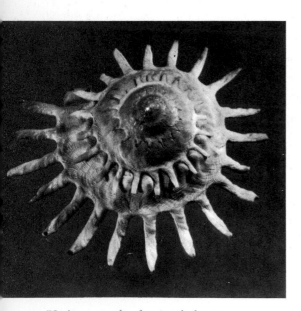

72 An example of nature's fantasy, *Stellaria solaris*, from the Andaman islands

passion for conchology, leaves an invalid god-daughter a collection of shells and, tied up with it, a large fortune, providing the girl reacts as Miss Crabbe hopes she will. Miss Poppy is only seventeen when her god-mother dies. The shell cabinets arrive with a sealed letter, the contents of which only the family lawyer and Miss Poppy's father, the rector of the village, are permitted to read. The clauses are as follows: on her twenty-first birthday, if Miss Poppy, from sheer love of science, has added only a few shells to the collection, she is to inherit the whole of Miss Crabbe's fortune; if on the other hand she takes no interest in the shells, she is to receive only a small legacy of five hundred pounds while the remainder of the fortune is to go to some charity specified in the will. The Rev. Merton is not allowed to divulge a word of this to his daughter, nor give her any advice on the subject. As might be expected Miss Poppy, innocent of the contents of the letter, and always having believed herself to be an heiress, greets the shell cabinets with a fine show of tears. But things improve as the novel progresses; a handsome young man interests her in the shells, while the reader, of course, learns quite a few interesting facts about the molluscan world. It is the parson who supplies the drama. Distracted by the situation he starts walking in his sleep and during one of his night prowls steals the *gloria-maris* out of its secret drawer. The shock on discovering the theft galvanizes the household and has the effect of bringing the paralyzed Miss Poppy to her feet. The young man by this time is madly in love with her and the fortune ensured. Miss Poppy, an intelligent young Victorian, has become thoroughly addicted to conchology; when she opens the will, the cabinets are bursting with new shells.

I will not attempt to describe *gloria-maris* for the coloured plate shows what a remarkably handsome shell it is. The British Museum owns five specimens: the one photographed here [figure 57] belonged originally to the Duke of Calonne and was brought over to England previous to the French Revolution. It came into the possession of the third Lord Tankerville and on the sale of his Museum in 1825 was bought by W. J. Broderip, a lawyer and well-known naturalist. This, at least, is the official story, but there is more to it than this. George Sowerby, the eminent conchologist, had charge of the Tankerville collection sale and being a friend of Broderip advised the lawyer what price, in his opinion, the *gloria-maris* would fetch. On hearing the figure of a hundred pounds, Broderip vowed he would never give such a sum for any shell, and yet being excessively desirous to possess this treasure, left a bid of £ 99 19s. 6d. His tiresome quibbling lost him the *gloria maris* which went for a hundred guineas. But as luck would have it, luck anyway for Broderip, the person who became the proud possessor of the coveted prize went bankrupt a short while afterwards, and when in its turn his collection went to the hammer, Broderip got his *gloria-maris* for fifty pounds. The Broderip collection was ultimately purchased by the British Museum.

There are numerous rarer cones than the *gloria-maris*, but we only have the space to deal with one of them here, the handsome *clytospira* of which there are only nine known specimens in the world [figure 74]. It is much rarer, in fact, than the *gloria-maris* and for some strange reason practically unknown to the general public. Its distribution seems to be world-wide in tropical waters, as it is known to come from the Gulf of Oman, Bombay, Japan, Aden and Mauritius. Two specimens taken near Bombay were found stuck to a ship's cable that had been drawn up from forty-five fathoms. The sailor who found them said that there had been originally three, but that the third and larger shell had dropped off as he reached over to gather them in. As will be seen from the photograph, one of its distinguishing features is its especially elevated spire.

There are five species of cones which are known to cause severe and even fatal stings to human beings: *Conus aulicus*, a pale or dark brown shell flecked with triangles of white running from the flattened spire to the base of the cone in horizontal drifts, sometimes crowded together so as to give the appearance of two encircling bands. The second, *Conus textile*, is a khaki yellow colour, marked with dark brown wavy lines running diagonally, with across it the same triangular points which are characteristic of certain species of cones. *Conus marmoreus* is also brown, but this time marbled with larger very white flecks. *Conus geographus* [figure 60] is a dark chocolate brown with white flecks; and finally we come to *Conus tulipa*, its markings being smudged brown and white with an underlay of pink, the whole crossed over by spotted lines. I chose *Conus geographus* as an illustration because this specimen is known to have been responsible for a man's death.

These poison cones are armed with a long fleshy proboscis which can be protruded well beyond the edge of

73 These cones are collectors' favourites. Engravings from the *Tableau Encyclopédique et Méthodique*

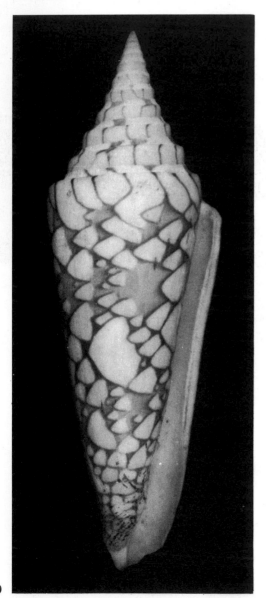

74 The exceedingly rare and beautiful *Conus clytospira*. This specimen comes from Mauritius

the shell. It is a pointed organ having a number of barbs, or radular teeth, each of which has a venom gland at its base. The animal normally uses it as a form of hypodermic needle with which to paralyze its prey, but if handled carelessly can turn it into a formidable weapon of defence. A jab in the hand from this weapon can have serious results and is capable of causing partial paralysis, or even death. A fatality from this source occurred in 1935 on Hayman Island, on the Great Barrier Reef. A visitor was carrying one of the shells when the proboscis pierced his hand; a little later symptoms of poisoning developed and he was rushed to the mainland, but too late, for he died before reaching hospital. Rumphius reports another case of a female slave dying at Banda. Surgeon Hinde RN saw a native of a small island in the New Briton group who had been stung by a *Conus geographus*. Immediately the man took a sharp stone and made small incisions all over his arm and shoulder, letting the blood flow freely. The native explained that had he not taken this precaution, he would certainly have died. People who have been stung and have recovered, describe the sensation they experience as being very painful; a kind of sharp burning under the skin.

The family *Cypraeidae* is as numerous as the *Conidae* and possibly the favourite among shell collectors. It is hard to resist their polished enamel surface and their beautiful colour patterns. There is also something particularly beguiling about their shape. They are globular and round and instinctively one reaches out to pick them up. One wants to hold them, to run one's fingers over their slippery, shiny surface, just as the Chinese carried lumps of jade or ivory around with them, using them as objects to caress with their fingers in much the same way as a pianist keeps a suppleness of touch by practising scales on the piano. The Chinese claimed that it developed the tactile senses so important to them in handling their beautiful porcelains.

Perry tells us that the cowry's scientific name originates from the circumstances of a shell of this genus having been presented to the temple of Aphrodite in Cyprus; and indeed, as he says, 'the beauty and splendour of these shells render them worthy of being offered at the shrine of the Goddess of Beauty'. Besides being beautiful, there is something in the quiet, unaggressive way they spend their lives that is most restful.

The cowry appears in all the warmer seas of the globe;

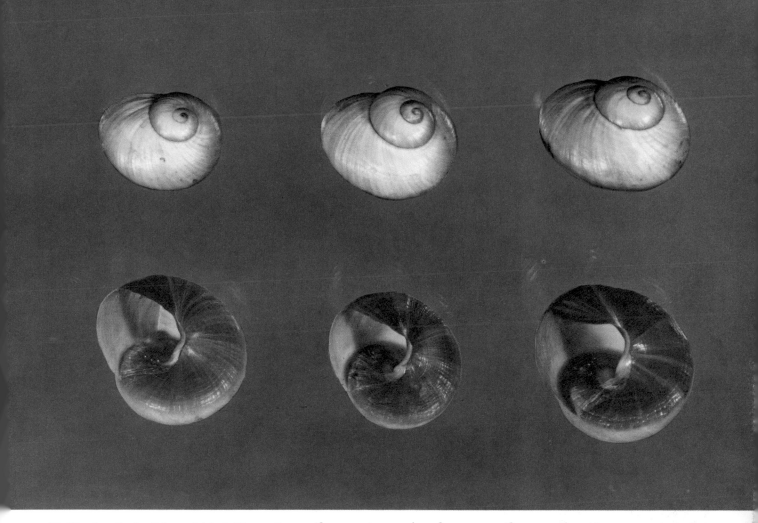

the great cowries, however, the popular tiger cowry and the rare orange cowry and the still rarer *guttata* and the beautiful *valentia* are all natives of tropical regions, delighting in warm climates. They are shy creatures and crawl slowly, browsing on weeds, and are seldom met with in the day-time for they usually remain concealed under rocks or hidden away in crevices amongst the coral with their bodies completely withdrawn inside the shell. It is at night, when they come out to feed, that one should see them, and it is advisable to carry a light of some form when hunting them, for the molluscs are even more striking in appearance than the shells they have fashioned. Joyce Allen, the Curator of Mollusca in Sydney's Australian Museum, describes them very well for us in her *Cowry Shells of World Seas*. Snail-like in appearance, they have a crawling foot and an ample covering mantle, or skin, formed by two prominent fleshy lobes that extend up, one on each side of the shell's back, and are capable of

61

76 The animal of the *Cypraea tigris* is even more striking in appearance than the shell it fashions

77 *Conus geographus*, one of the five species of cones known to cause severe, or even fatal, stings

completely hiding the shell from view when crawling or gliding among the coral reefs. In most species this mantle is beautifully mottled and heavily ornamented with branched or pointed filaments that wave about sensitively in the water. As in all other molluscs, these mantles are responsible for the secretion of the shell, and meeting as they do along the back, enveloping the whole shell, they guard it from attack by encrusting organisms and preserve the brilliant enamel surface indefinitely [figure 76]. Even England's small native cowry is a beautiful creature to look at, having a dark vermilion proboscis and yellowish red tentacles, spotted with yellow. The upper part of the foot is striated longitudinally with yellow and brown, and the mantle is greenish brown, edged with brownish red.

The best known and most popular of the cowries is the *Cypraea tigris*. One wonders, though, why it should be called tiger, for its spots resemble much more those of a leopard. The shell of this cowry grows to a length of about four inches and is one of the most beautiful in spite of its being one of the commonest of all molluscs, and among other things, it was, along with the *Cypraea mauritania*, an invariable choice of the eighteenth-century silversmiths when making up their shell snuff-boxes. One usually finds this cowry in pairs, a fact I constantly witnessed myself while on the Barrier Reef. The great Rumphius, usually so accurate, states that the *Cypraea* as a family are inedible. 'All that is smooth and shiny', he tells us, 'is no good for food, rough and spiky shells being always better.' I have eaten tiger cowries in Japan where they throw them on to hot coals and roast them. They tasted somewhat like oysters, though I must admit it hurt my feelings seeing so many beautiful shells being wasted. The Philippinos also eat the tiger cowry, but they dry it first and then fry it. In the Fiji Islands they cut the shell in half, place it round a stone with two or three showy olive shells at the sides and use it as a bait for cuttle-fish. They also weight their nets with them. In the past the Italians used them for burnishing paper and ironing lace. Gipsies are supposed to have been responsible for their wide distribution in Europe—gipsies, and one presumes, sailors.

All of us, I imagine, have certain objects that bring back vivid memories, and amongst my touchstones are the tiger cowries. They always evoke a scene I witnessed on the Island of Lamu, off the coast of Kenya, forgotten now and ignored, yet once the Zanzibar Sultanate's most

78 An engraving of a *Cypraea felina* from Martin Lister's *Historia Conchyliorum*

79 An engraving of *Cypraea vitellus* from Perry's *Conchology*

important *entrepôt* for gold, ivory, spices and slaves. The place fascinated me and my curiosity was amply repaid. Lamu still belongs to Zanzibar and the Sultan's red flag was flying from one of the crenellated towers of the Portuguese fort. The glare thrown off from the white-washed walls was terrific, nor did the polished brass cannons with which the place is defended obviate it. The whole thing looked like a fort from a Henty novel and would have been the delight of any small boy. When I visited it, the place was being used as a prison for Mau-Mau, and in one of the corner towers we came across the warders' wives seated cross-legged on the flat roof. Armed with long wires they were trying to clean out *Cypraea tigris*. Tenacious of life, the unfortunate animals were putting up a stout resistance and only came away in pieces, which necessitated much dipping of the shells into buckets of water. The women were from one of the coastal tribes, and as Mohammedans, were enveloped in black. Outlined against their brilliant background they had the appearance of enormous crows.

In her *Popular History of the Mollusca*, 1851, Mary Roberts describes cowries at different periods of their growth, stressing the changes of form, pattern and colour which each shell undergoes. So marked are they that it is hard at times to identify the particular family. In the *Cypraea mauritianus*, for example, the first tinting, in its primitive, or bulla form, is pale yellow with wavy bands; in a second stage the waves become agglomerated while the pale yellow ground changes to triangular flame-like spots. The teeth meanwhile are fully developed, and the sides are strengthened by means of a rich dark brown coating, thickly spread over the dorsal surface, forming irregular reticulations.

The most striking instance of gradual development, she tells us, occurs in the tiger cowry: I included it here since it reads like a set of quarterings thought up by some medieval College of Heralds. The colour, at first, is of a uniform chestnut bay, but afterwards seems to break into bands of close-set, waved blotches of a richer hue. A little later another coating is superimposed, and upon this is deposited a series of rather distant zigzag flames upon a white ground. Thirdly, the mollusc turns its attention towards the formation of teeth, and a few coloured spots become apparent round the outer side. In the next stage, a second layer of white enamel is added,

63

but considerably thinner and more delicate than the preceding, through which the previous zigzag are visible. Further dark spots are deposited. These again are overspread by a thin white coating, intermixed with numerous rich black and brown spots, showing for the first time a narrower dorsal line, mostly edged with reddish brown, having also the deposit of dark spots overspread with a bluish transparent milky hue.

We must not, however, dwell too long on the *Cypraea tigris*; many other species of this fascinating family claim our attention: for one, the lovely *Ovulum ovum*, or China shell, which is often pure white, sometimes ranging to pink, pale violet or yellow without any patterns or markings. Then there is the orange cowry or *Cypraea aurantium* [figure 61] which at one time commanded handsome sums on the market. It has always been considered very highly in the South Pacific and in Fiji and the New Hebrides is worn as a badge of rank by native chiefs—and indeed, one of the most remarkable Fijian industries is the working of whales' teeth to represent this cowry. As can be seen, the specimen shown in the coloured plate is a bright orange but sometimes the shell shades to pale buttercup yellow. Whatever the colour variations, however, the sides and the base of the cowry are always white. Joyce Allen in *Cowry Shells of World Seas* tells us that 'although it is difficult for the average collector to obtain a specimen of this graceful shell, it is not really so rare as one is inclined to believe, but its restricted range and the fact that it is a great favourite with the natives who seem disinclined to describe its habitat on the island reefs where it lives, make it a scarce and much desired trophy'.

Amongst the cowries the rarest are *Cypraea princeps* and *leucodon* [figure 83]. Of *Cypraea leucodon* there are only two known examples in the world, one belonging to the British Museum and the second specimen having recently turned up at the Harvard University Museum. The British Museum specimen shown here is photographed in black and white since it is not a particularly distinguished-looking shell, its markings being large creamy spots on a buff ground. What is remarkable about it, are its teeth. In no other species are they so pronounced. To add to its aura it is not known from where either of the two specimens of *Cypraea leucodon* originate. South Africa has been suggested as a likely place.

81 *Cypraea mappa*, so-called on account of its markings which resemble the contours of a map, from Perry's *Conchology*

82 The rare *Cypraea valentia* of which there are five, or perhaps six, known specimens in the world. From Perry's *Conchology*

Another shell about which there is considerable mystery is the *Cypraea valentia*, so named by Perry, who states in his description of it that it was obtained from Amboyna by Lord Valentia, a statement that was later proved to be incorrect. Although one of the earliest named shells, it is still one of the greatest marine rarities and uncertainty surrounds its habitat. There are five, or perhaps six, known specimens throughout the world and it is amazing that with so much subsequent diving and dredging, the shell has not been found in greater quantities. Miss Allen tells us that one of the specimens was for a short time in the possession of a private collector in Australia. He had purchased it from the captain of one of the pearl-shell trawlers, who recounts that he had originally possessed two of them, but having given them to his children to play with, one of them had got broken.

The *valentia* is a large shell with a swollen back and is very extravagantly marked [figure 82]. The base is yellowish in colour, faintly tinted with rose-pink, a shade which darkens as it mounts the shell, becoming golden yellow over the dorsum which is splashed with a large, red map-like area. The pink sides are spotted with dark purplish red.

We cannot leave this engrossing family without mentioning the small *Cypraea moneta* or Money cowry [figure 66]. As the plate shows, it is a small, oval, depressed shell; flat and white beneath with thick edges that darken to a yellowish-white, becoming pale lemon colour on the upper surface. To illustrate it here I have chosen some of the deeper yellow specimens, thinking it would make more of a display. It is an inhabitant of the Pacific Ocean and the Indian Sea from the Moluccas to the

83 Two views of *Cypraea leucodon*, of which there are only two known specimens in existence. This one is in the British Museum collection and the other is in the Harvard University Museum

84 *Cypraea mappa*

Atlantic Ocean. It can be found in enormous quantities in this area and large fortunes were made by European traders who transported them to the West Coast of Africa where they were traded for ivory, gold and slaves. A slave would be worth anything from twenty to fifty thousand shells. Official statistics inform us that in the year 1848 sixty tons of the money cowry were imported into Liverpool; and in the following year, four times as many. According to Reeve in his *Conchologia Iconica*, a gentleman residing at Cuttack is said to have paid for the erection of his bungalow entirely in cowries. The building cost him about four hundred pounds, which in cowries amounted to sixteen million shells. The common method of handling the cowries was by threading them on a string, forty cowries to one string.

Nowadays the Gold Coast has its own currency and only in out-of-the-way places are shells used for barter. Shell currency, however, has been in use from a very remote age and the habit dies hard. The little *Cypraea moneta* is still a symbol of power, and chieftains still sew them into their regalia and regard them as essential ornaments for their person. The riches they once commanded may have diminished but they are still millionaires in terms of shells and they are proud to show them off.

The *Cypraea moneta* has one distinguishing feature which singles it out from other shell currency: it is used entire and not made out of portions of shells, thus requiring a certain amount of labour in the process of formation. Among the tribes of the north-west coast of America, the common *Dentalium indianorum* or tusk shell used to form the standard of values, until it was superseded under the auspices of the Hudson Bay Company by blankets. Wampum is even better known as shell money and seems to have been current along the whole seaboard of North America from Maine to Florida as well as among the inland tribes east of the Mississippi. The tusk shell used to be turned and worked and sewn into strips, while wampum consisted of strings of cylindrical beads, each about a quarter of an inch in length and half that in breadth. The size was regulated by early European settlers who also adapted it to their own use. It was fashioned from the clam shell *Mercenaria mercenaria*, commonly called quahog. The purple beads made from the lip of the shell were more valuable than the white beads made from the body and when polished looked like amethyst.

Interesting Shells

85 *Argaria imperialis*

86 (*opposite*) A plate of variously-coloured *Pectinidae*, from Küster's *Conchylien Cabinet*, Nuremberg, 1857

IN THE PREVIOUS CHAPTER we dealt with the actual formation of a shell, giving, at the same time, a few details concerning different families or *genera*. Now, irrespective of their classes, let us look at a few of the more exceptional molluscs, which every collector would like to possess. We will turn at will from univalve to bivalve, the choice being far too bewildering to take them in an ordered scientific manner.

The great *Strombus gigas* or fountain shell of the West Indies is one of the largest shells, weighing sometimes as much as four or five pounds [figure 87]. Strombs are found in the West Indies, the Indian and Pacific Oceans, the Mediterranean and the Red Sea. They are solid conical shells with expanded apertures, yet despite their cumbersome appearance they are surprisingly agile and have the power of executing astonishing leaps. These leaps are accomplished by a stout clam-like door, or *operculum*, which the animal digs into the sand, using it in much

87 *Strombus gigas* or Fountain shell, from an unpublished plate by P. L. Duclos, 1835. This shows the clam-like door or *operculum* with which the animal accomplishes astonishing leaps. Its eyes are clearly visible

the same way as a pole vaulter uses his pole. Hugh Cuming, the famous nineteenth-century collector, recounts how, on one occasion, he lost a beautiful specimen by the animal suddenly leaping into the water while he was admiring it. If one happens to be in a glass-bottomed boat one can sometimes catch sight of them, rocking and swaying to their jerky movements, like a parade of circus elephants. One has to be very cautious, however, regarding one's approach, for they have a singular quickness of vision. They are also reported to have a very keen sense of smell, but there is no proof of this.

The *Strombus gigas* is carnivorous in its habits and is fairly easy to find since it lives upon sandy drifts at the bottom of the sea in comparatively shallow water. Pink pearls are obtained from the giant conch of the West Indies and a large quantity of shells are annually imported from the Bahamas for the manufacture of cameos. The secret of cameo cutting simply consists in knowing that the inner strata of porcelainous shells is differently coloured from the exterior. Once cut, the pale upper portion, or coating, stands out in relief against the red-brown of the lower layer. The best shells for cameo engraving are the *Cassis rufa* and the *Cassis cornuta*; the *Cassis cornuta* being white on an orange ground and *Cassis rufa* pale salmon coloured or orange. The *Strombus gigas* is yellow or pink. In the Barbados, the *Strombus gigas* still furnishes a favourite repast for the natives and in Santa Cruz they have used the shells for paving the streets.

We move from this large, heavy shell to one of the most fragile of all molluscs, the delicate little violet snail or *Ianthina* [figure 75]. 'It is probable', remarks Captain Cook of this animal, 'that it never goes down to the bottom, nor willingly approaches any shore, for its shell is exceedingly brittle.' The great explorer was quite correct in his observation, for it is, indeed, pelagic or floating, and drifts about freely over the surface of the sea, and is often found in mid-Atlantic in wandering islands of Gulf weed. After a severe storm it is sometimes cast up on the shores of the west coast of Ireland and Scotland: it is not, however, an inhabitant of northern climes, but drifts about on warm currents such as the Gulf Stream. These creatures, as the coloured plate shows, produce almost transparent shells, which range from pale lilac to deep purple. As if conscious of their delicate colourings and their fragile appearance, the *Ianthina* are sometimes to be found in groups living upon colonies of *Physalia*, a kind of jelly fish more commonly known as Portuguese men-o'-war. There is often yet another creature, a little crustacean who establishes himself on the raft of *Ianthina*. It also assumes the brilliant blue colour of the mollusc. The question of the raft is another strange detail about the shell. In order to steady its floating position in the sea, the creature fabricates a kind of raft by the excretion of slime in which it imprisons air bubbles. The mucus soon hardens and thus forms a tough, strong float on which the creature moves from place to place.

The *Scalaria pretiosa* or wentletrap was at one time considered a great rarity and was much prized by collectors on account of its strange and beautiful appearance [figures 88, 91]. A good specimen, in former days, sold for over a hundred pounds or two hundred and eighty dollars but the shell is no longer scarce. Good specimens now only fetch shillings. The *Scalaria pretiosa* is found off the coast of China; and the Chinese discovering a ready market for these precious shells used to make a clever imitation from rice flour paste, a fraud that was only found out when a collector, wishing to clean his specimens, dipped one into water and discovered that it began to melt.

I think I am correct in claiming that the *Scalaria pretiosa* is the only shell which has detached whorls: they do not touch each other and are only connected by small ribs, curious ridges which cross each whorl at regular intervals and serve as buttresses. A fine specimen of this shell ought to be semi-transparent and of a light brown colour tinged with rose. The ribs are opaque white. Its common name, wentletrap, is a corruption of the German *Wendeltreppe* or winding staircase. The *genus* is supposed to resemble a staircase, hence the Latin name, *Scalaria*.

Having discussed two of the most fragile shells, we now turn, for contrast, to the large *Charonia tritonis*, or triton shell, a well-known shell and one of the most handsome in the sea [figure 80]. It can measure about a foot in length and seven or eight inches in diameter at the mouth which swells out in a pleasing baroque way. Its ample whorls, mounting in a long elegant spire, are marked by encircling ribs striped in white, yellow and brown, mixed by the creature's mantle into rows of moon-shaped blotches. Everyone has doubtless seen this agate-like shell reproduced in paintings, more often than not doing service as a horn being blown by different sea deities. Rubens uses

88 The curious and much sought-after *Scalaria pretiosa*, or *Epitoneum scalare*, found off the coast of China

it thus when he shows us Marie de Medici landing on French soil amidst a welter of stiff ruffs and rich brocades. The great *Charonia tritonis* is a native of the West Indies and of the Pacific Ocean and is the conch shell used by the Polynesian islanders as a war trumpet.

Captain Cook remarks that during his visit to the islands, he never knew the blowing of the conch amongst the natives to portend good: it always seemed to be signal of a hostile attack. William Ellis, the missionary, informs us,

89 Three specimens of *Harpa ventricosa* from Mauritius

however, in his *Polynesian Researches*, 1832, that these conches were not only used in war to stimulate the warriors into action, but were also blown 'when a procession walked to the temple, or at the inauguration of the King, during the worship at the temple, or when a taboo or restriction was imposed in the name of the Gods.' Specimens of these shells mounted as trumpets may be seen in the ethnographical section of any good museum. In order to facilitate their blowing the islanders make a perforation, about an inch in diameter, near the apex of the shell Into this they insert a bamboo cane about three feet in length which is secured by binding it to the shell with fine braid; the aperture is rendered air-tight by cementing the outside with a resinous gum from the bread-fruit tree. Early travellers record that the noise of these trumpets being blown from the platforms on the large war canoes was far more terrific than that of the drum. *Charonia*

90 Various specimens of *Tellina*. The central shell is *Tellina coccinea*, surrounded by *Tellina radiata*, from Florida

tritonis was also used on the sugar plantations of the West Indies to summon the slaves to work, and the Voodoos of Haiti blow on it in their ceremonies. A species somewhat similar to the *Charonia tritonis* is found in the Mediterranean. I have heard it being used by fishermen when sailing into Corfu Harbour; it has a loud, monotonous, yet melancholy sound.

The harp shells comprise a small but beautiful group of

91 *Scalaria pretiosa*, or wentletrap. The Chinese used to make clever forgeries of this shell from rice-flour paste to sell to collectors

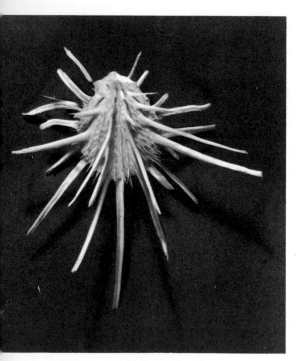

92 The snow-white and spiky *Spondylus imperialis* from China. In its mature state the spines of this shell encourage marine growth of all kinds to stick to it, thus camouflaging its exact whereabouts

molluscs, and are distinguished chiefly by their ribs which cover the whole external part of the shell, running longitudinally like pleats in a dress. They are found in Ceylon, Mauritius and the Philippine Islands, 'and may be regarded', writes Perry, 'as one of the most laboured of Nature's works, as they present to the eye many little circumstances of high finishing and painting, which an artist can by no means easily imitate, or convey to the mind by any laboured description whatever'. The *Harpa ventricosa* not only possesses a beautiful shell but also glories in a vermilion skin [figure 89].

In Mauritius this shell is caught with lines baited with small pieces of flesh. Troops garrisoned there used to employ much of their leisure in fishing for harps and olives. 'It is the amusement of the place', wrote Broderip in about 1830, 'to watch over the trim apparatus of lines hung over some sand bank to tempt the various brilliant species of olives which there abound, or to wait for the more rare appearance of the harp shell, till the rich hues of its inhabitants are seen glowing through the clear water, in the rays of a tropical rising sun.'

The most familiar bivalve is the oyster, found in the temperate and tropical seas all over the world, and of which nearly a hundred species have been described. I have seen beaches in Australia littered with the refuse of the ordinary *Ostrea edulis*: they lay, bleached by sunshine and rain to the colour of snow. The Greeks and Romans valued oysters very highly and their epicures spared neither trouble nor expense to procure those which they considered had the finest flavour. They shipped them from the Dardanelles, from the Adriatic, from the Bay of Cumae and from England, and relished most those which were brought from different lands, and afterwards fattened in the Lucrine Lake. Lentulus says that the oyster is an animal 'so disagreeable and nauseous in appearance, whether seen in the shell or out of it, that he must be considered a bold man who first moved it to his lips'. According to Suetonius, the Roman general who defeated Queen Boadicea in 61 AD, Britain enjoyed a certain reputation for the pearls found in her mussels, sufficient reputation for it to form one of the attractions which induced Julius Caesar to undertake his expedition to her shores. Pliny tells us that the quest was not altogether a success so far as quality was concerned, although Caesar did obtain a sufficient quantity to cover a buckler which he dedicated to Venus Genitrix.

Most of the bivalves hare fewer literary connections; among them the beautiful *Spondylus* or thorny oyster. I mention this for we have a coloured plate of the *Spondylus cumingii* from Japan [figure 18] and a black and white photograph of *Spondylus imperialis* from China [figure 92]. Here too we find an enormous family with sixty-eight species already described. Few of the bivalves have been esteemed 'fancy shells' or have commanded high prices; nevertheless, some of the *Spondylus* are very beautiful. They have a regular shell with divergent ribs terminating in foliaceous spines. The spines rising from the ribs vary considerably in length and thickness in individuals of the same species—colour is also extremely variable, characteristics that do little to help in identification. In its mature state the spiny nature of the *Spondylus* encourages marine growth of all kinds to adhere to it, thus camouflaging the exact whereabouts of these brilliantly coloured bivalves. They are almost impossible to find in the coral reefs to which they anchor themselves. A good specimen today fetches from twelve to fifteen pounds, or about thirty-five dollars.

Structurally related to the *Spondylidae* are the *Pectinidae*; they are what one might call their ambulatory cousins. The *Spondylidae* are usually fixed to a substratum of rock or coral, while the *Pecten* or scallop swims through the water in a zigzag course made by a series of sudden contractions of the two valves of its shell [figure 86]. The famous French naturalist Cuvier calls them the butterflies of the ocean, not as he well might have done, however, because of their erratic movements, nor from the fact that when their two valves are expanded, they in some respects resemble the wings of our summer insects, but on account of the various and beautiful colours they exhibit. These attractively sculptured shells boast of the most amazing varieties of colours; brilliant reds and yellows and oranges, brown clouded with violet, or pale blue speckled with green. There is no end to the variety they display. If one were to collect only one genus of shell, it is certainly the *Pecten* one would specialize in.

There are several entertaining stories regarding the agility of scallops, for these animals possess the power of leaping to a considerable distance. Lesson, the Swedish naturalist, says that he has seen them leaping out of the water by striking their valves rapidly together. When

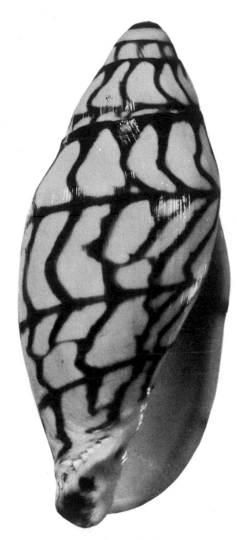

93 The handsome *Voluta bednalli brazier*

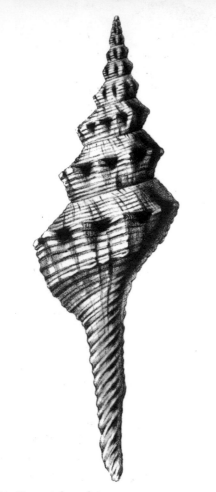

94 *Fusus tuberculatus*

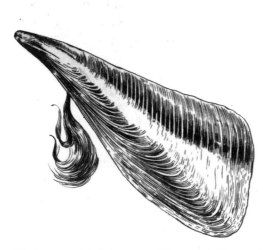

95 A pen-and-ink drawing of the great *Pinna*, showing the *byssus* from which material used to be woven

stranded by the tide, they will also tumble forward by the same kind of movement, until they have regained the water. In his *Fauna of Greenland*, the Danish entomologist Fabricius wrote about a northern species called *Pecten islandicus*. The natives used it as food but had difficulty in cooking it, for the shell, put into the pot alive, often leapt out of it again. There is also the fascinating story of the *Trigonia pectinata*, the fossil shell of the Jurassic Seas, and although it is not of the *Pectinidae* family, it is at least a bivalve and so we can include it here. The first living specimen was obtained by Stutchbury while dredging in Sydney Harbour. The *Cambridge Natural History* reports the episode very graphically: picking the shell out of the net, Stutchbury placed it in the bow of the small boat that was rowing him around, remarking to a companion that it must be a *Trigonia*. His companion laughed at the idea, reminding him that all known *Trigonia* were fossils. Suddenly the shell in question took a smart leap into the sea, thus baffling any further effort to discover its generic position. It was three months before Stutchbury succeeded in obtaining another specimen.

Another interesting bivalve is the *Pinna*. Although not a particularly beguiling shell to look at, the large species is handsome and sometimes attains a length of two feet. For its size the shell is remarkably thin and brittle, almost transparent and of a tortoiseshell brown with a slight nacreous flush inside. This shell is unusually interesting because a silky material can be made from the *byssus* which it spins itself [figure 95]. The *byssus*, I must explain, is a fine silky filament by which the bivalve attaches itself to the surface of rocks. The great *Pinna* excels any other mollusc in the quantity and fineness of its silk and it was these long strands that the Romans started weaving into articles of dress. A robe of this material is mentioned by Procopius as the gift of a Roman emperor to the Satrap of Armenia, and in the year 1754 a pair of stockings were presented to Pope Benedict XV. So fine were they that the gift was enclosed in a silver snuff box! Until quite recently, the inhabitants of Sicily and Calabria were still weaving this material. Mixing it with about one-third of real silk, they knitted it into gloves, capes and even garments of much larger size. They were supposed to be very soft and wonderfully warm, but were naturally far too expensive to be anything but objects of curiosity. I have seen some gloves made of this material and they

96 A collection of *Trochidae*. The large central shell is *Trochus niloticus*, from a plate in Küster's *Conchylien Cabinet*, Nuremberg, 1875

were of a brownish yellow colour with a slight sheen to them, resembling the varnished, gilded hue one finds on the back of some beetles.

Many of the bivalves have the power of burying themselves deep in the sands on which they live; the *Solen* or razor shell, for instance, is capable of burying itself as much as five feet under the surface, rendering its capture almost impossible. The animal is sometimes eaten by the inhabitants of seaside places and is considered very highly as bait. One species, the *Solen siliqua*, is so much in request that the Irish have a song, which they sing in chorus,

97 *Turritella terebra*

98 *Trichotropis bicarinata*

when they go out to catch it. It is taken at low tide by plunging a slender iron rod into the sand. Ann Pratt in *Chapters on the Common Things of the Sea Coast*, 1853, describes the hunting: 'the slight motion of the sand, made by the foot, sufficiently alarms the fish to induce it to throw out jets of water, or it would lie secure enough, for the holes are not often easily discovered. In some cases salt is thrown into the cavity, which so irritates the fish, that it immediately comes to the surface; but the eye must be watchful, and the hand must be ready, as if not seized instantly, it plunges down again and no subsequent irritation from the salt will induce it to come out to face further danger.'

But of all the boring mollusca, the *Pholas*, and the *Teredo* or ship worms are the most active. Eschewing the sand they bury themselves in rocks, marble, sandstone and wood, the softest material they would consider being hard clay.

Take to begin with the *Pholas* or piddocks, commonly known in America as angels' wings [figure 99]. *Pholas* is derived from the Greek *Pholeo*, to bore, and they are well named for they live and die buried in the hollows they make for themselves in the rocks. Considering their nature one would expect them to have sturdy, thick shells, but this is not at all the case, most of them being frail and delicate and some almost transparent. I am holding one up now, as I write, the *Phola costata*, an American species. It is a beautiful shell, bone white and looks as if it were fashioned out of starched piqué linen.

For years naturalists were perplexed about the means these delicate mollusca employed for penetrating such solid substances and eventually after much hesitation it was decided that the animal exuded a powerful chemical solution which helped dissolve the rock. But even now not all naturalists are agreed on this point. One weapon, however, all *Pholas* have in common, and this is a sharp series of spines which run along the outsplaying ribs of the shell, and it is quite obvious that penetration is achieved by the expansion and contraction of the powerful adductor muscle which causes the toothed shell valves to rasp away the surface of the rock. Traces of this rasping can frequently be seen on the walls of the animal's furrow.

Like many denizens of the sea, the *Phola* becomes phosphorescent at night, and on warm summer evenings one can see a bluish-white light shining in the mysterious

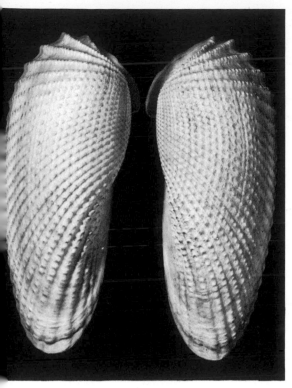

99 *Phola costata*, known as Angel's wings in America, becomes phosphorescent at night

100 The municipal wharf-house at Benicia, California, after it collapsed in 1920 through the activity of *Teredo navalis* or large sea worm

depths of the rock. So strong is the phosphorescent liquor emitted by this animal that it illumines whatever it touches, and Dr Priestly in his *History of Light* tells us that even the mouth of the person who eats it glows with a strange glimmer. His statement is borne out by Reaumur and Beccarius, two French eighteenth-century naturalists, who made a special study of phosphoric light. 'A single *Phola*', they write, 'will render a pint of milk so beautifully luminous that surrounding objects are clearly visible in its aura.'

Active the *Pholas* may be, but their exploits pale in comparison with the havoc perpetrated by the *Teredo navalis*, or large ship worm. It has been known and feared as a menace to wooden structures ever since it was first recorded by the Greek philosopher and naturalist Theophrastus in 300 BC. One reads that the giant *Teredo* is capable of making a burrow a yard long measuring two inches in diameter at its widest part. Small wonder that sailors have such a healthy respect for it. The combined efforts of hundreds of *Teredo* have been known to destroy many a proud vessel. The 'wooden walls of England' were subject to constant attack until the ships were lined with copper bottoms. History tells us that it was responsible for toppling the proud temple of Serapis into the water. Serapis was the Greek god of the underworld and his temple stood out to sea on a promontory just north of Naples. One can well believe this story when one looks at the photograph of the Municipal Wharf House of Benicia in California which collapsed in 1920 through the activity of this terrible worm [figure 100]. During the eighteenth century it was also known to have threatened whole districts in Holland and only the timely discovery of the mischief these creatures have wrought in the piles supporting the dikes saved the situation.

The shell of the *Teredo* is smaller and thinner than that of the *Pholas*, but to make up for this the animal is equipped with sharp chisel-like jaws with which it cuts its way into the wood. In directing its course it generally excavates to coincide with the grain of the wood, but there are instances where it crosses it, even when working in the hardest teak. While making these excavations it lines them with a shelly substance which gradually forms into a tube, the animal occupying that part which is most deeply sunken in the timber.

Most people hope to include the following shells in their

79

collections, for they are the most spectacular; among them are the delicate *Tellinidae* from Florida, which are tinted a deep orange-yellow shading to palest saffron near the edge [figure 90]. Crossed over with radiating bands of rose each shell gives the effect of a sunrise. There are the *Haliotidae* or abalones from California with ther brilliant, dark-green lining of pearly nacre, a shell that exists the world over, known under different names. There are the *Trochidae*, one of which is pyramidal in shape and vividly striped white and crimson with a highly nacreous inner surface valued in the button trade [figure 96]. There is the large globular tunshell and the pointed, slender auger, correctly known as *Terebra*, which is flecked brown and white like a regularly marked tortoiseshell [figure 75]. There are the *Mitridae*, equally pointed, not quite so elegant perhaps, but often marked with bright vermilion spots, a rare colour in shells. The olives or *Olividae* are also a numerous family, all cylindrical, all highly polished and often very prettily marked, a great favourite always with collectors [figure 117]. It is when I come to the volutes or *Volutidae* that I must pause for a minute. They are a tropical shell numbering about a hundred species, among them the comparatively rare *Maculopeplum junonia* from the Mexican Gulf [figure 101], still a great favourite with American collectors and then—and this is the reason for our pause—the extraordinary *Voluta musica* figure 104]. No two of these shells are marked alike, and looking at the arrangement of the lines running through the specimens shown here in the illustration, it is easy to understand why it should have been named the musical volute. The lines look like bars printed on sheet music and the black dots with which they are peppered like notes. So clearly indicated are they at times that one might almost play them. What, one wonders, would the music be? The ordered cadences of Handel's *Water Music*, or some liquid complaint from the deep.

It is with regret that I come to the last shell on our list—the *Turbinella pyrum* or sacred chank [figure 115]. For some weeks now I have been working with these twisted, lovely creatures from the sea, looking, sorting, deciding which shells to describe, wondering if I should ever be able to capture their beauty, and yet anxious, at the same time, not to explain away the sense of mystery which surrounds them:

101 The brown-spotted *Maculopeplum junonia* found only off the coast of southern Florida. Before the days of dredging, it was considered a great prize; and even now that it is less scarce, it is still eagerly sought-after

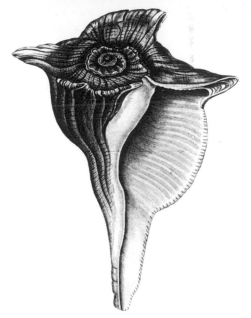

I wiped away the weeds and foam,
I fetched my sea-born treasures home;
But the poor, unsightly, noisome things
Had left their beauty on the shore,
With the sun and the sand and the wild uproar.

But when Emerson wrote these lines he was certainly thinking of a more ephemeral cargo than shells.

There is no reason why the *Turbinella pyrum* or chank should have waited till the last, for it is by no means the most extraordinary of our molluscs. It is just a question of chance. Its real interest lies in its connection with the Hindus and its association with their god Vishnu. It is a heavy shell and somewhat pear-shaped to look at, ranging from white to a creamy beige. It is fished in quantities off the southernmost tip of India, in the Gulf of Manaar; in fact it used to constitute one of Ceylon's major exports.

When in India a few years ago, I visited the great temples in the South, a complication of sculptured pylons towering above the coconut palms. It was in their dark, smoke-blackened halls that I remember seeing my first representations of Vishnu. He is generally shown four-armed, holding his usual attributes, a lotus flower, a sort of discus or sharp-edged missile weapon dancing with

102 An engraving from the *Tableau Encyclopédique et Méthodique*

103 The handsome *Voluta imperialis*

flames when whirled by Vishnu, a mace or club, and the chank which is used as a trumpet conferring victory on whoever should sound it. The chank has a deeper signification than this, but I never was able to find anyone to explain it to me. There is also a sinistral form of the chank, which is excessively rare and regarded with extraordinary veneration. The priests in the temples use it for administering medicine and often one will find it elaborately carved or inlaid with gold and precious stones [figure 115]. Perhaps it should be explained that the twist of the spine in nearly all univalves is dextral, or from left to right, the shell in this case being placed towards the observer and its mouth downwards. The chank proving an exception to this usual formation is no doubt the reason for the veneration in which it is held. I find also that the chank appears as the symbol on the coins of some of the ancient Indian empires and until quite recently was still retained on a coinage of the Rajah of Travancore.

There is one last detail concerning molluscs in general, and that is the question of their life span. Naturalists know very little about the subject, or seem unwilling to commit themselves to any definite statement; five to eight years, however, would appear to be the average expectancy. Some of the bivalves are only a year in coming to maturity while the gasteropods, as a whole, are slow in maturing. The longest lived, the Methuselah of the molluscs, in all probability is the giant clam, and that may be a centenarian. There is the well-known story of the British Museum snail, and although a land mollusc, I think it can be told here, for it is such a remarkable example of hibernation, and I give the exact dates as they appear in the official report. On 25 March 1846, two specimens of *Eremina desertorium*, collected by Charles Lamb in Egypt some time previously, were fixed upon tablets and placed in the collection among the other molluscs of the Museum. Four years later, having occasion to examine some shells in the same case as the snails, the curator noticed a recently formed epiphragm over the mouth of one of the animals, an epiphragm being a secretion of slime with which snails usually seal up their shell. Removing the animals from the tablet he placed them in tepid water. Much to the curator's surprise one of them came out of its shell, and the next day ate some cabbage leaves. A month or two afterwards it began repairing the lip of its shell, which had been broken when it was first affixed to the tablet.

104 Three specimens of *Voluta musica*, showing the lines which look like sheet-music and the black dots which resemble notes

The Great Barrier Reef

105 An engraving by Redouté from the *Tableau Encyclopédique et Méthodique*

106 Hugh Cuming (1791-1865), perhaps the greatest shell-collector there has ever been. An engraving from Lovell Reeve's *Conchologia Iconica*

THE GREAT BARRIER REEF, along with the Philippines, is probably the most auspicious area in the world for shells. About a hundred thousand different species of molluscs exist; out of these about ten thousand occur on and around the reefs of Queensland's coast. I would like to try to recapture for other collectors, therefore, a little of the excitement one experiences on an actual shell-gathering expedition, at the same time giving a few practical hints. Before embarking on my own modest expedition, I would like to mention possibly the greatest shell collector of all times, a remarkable and little-known man called Hugh Cuming [figure 106]. It is difficult, even impossible, to write about shell collecting without referring to him, for his career is of interest to all collectors.

Very little has been written on Hugh Cuming. It is known that he designed his own ship, a fast sailing clipper which he fitted out with all the equipment necessary to a professional naturalist. He sailed in her, we know, to the islands of the South Pacific, and on another voyage explored the west coast of South America. A third expedition included the Philippines. In fact he spent the major part of his life collecting shells, and I would say that most of the valuable specimens now in the British Museum were from his collection. His own cabinets contained nearly twenty thousand species and varieties, and many of his specimens were illustrated by G. B. Sowerby in his *Thesaurus Conchyliorum* and in Lovell Reeve's *Conchologia Iconica*. Other works were also based on his collection; indeed, the material he brought back and exhibited in his London house in Gower Street kept naturalists occupied for over fifty years.

These are the generally known facts about Cuming and it was quite some time before I could find any further material concerning him. By luck, one day, I came across an essay by Lovell Reeve which I found in a book entitled *Portraits of Men of Eminence* and it was from this work that I gathered these further details.

Cuming's clipper was named *Discoverer* and we know

that on her maiden voyage she visited the Society Islands, stopping on the way at Pitcairn, colonized by the descendants of Christian and Young, two of the mutineers of the *Bounty*. At Tahiti we hear of him becoming an intimate friend of Queen Pomaré. 'The rich conchological novelties that now rewarded Mr Cuming's toil in dredging, wandering and wading, induced him to spend upwards of a twelvemonth in the various little known islands of this wide expanse of ocean, especially the coral reef islands, many of which had not been hitherto visited by any naturalist.' He returned to Valparaiso laden with spoils.

His second voyage along the west coast of South America was of even longer duration than the first. He spent nearly two years dredging, hunting and exploring. He must have been a man of considerable charm, for the Chilean Government seemed to have granted him every facility. He was never asked for harbour dues and the inhabitants of every port he visited seem to have turned out to do him honour.

Eventually, after twelve years abroad he returned to England, the hold of his clipper laden with treasures. For many an evening to come the Zoological Society meetings were to be enlivened by the brilliant displays of his shells. But the excitement of collecting had so gripped him that long before his conchological novelties were exhausted Cuming was off again, this time to the Philippines.

Cuming spent four years altogether out in the Philippines, and returned to England in 1839 where he remained until he died twenty-six years later, 'occupying himself', as Reeve writes, 'in arranging and completing his collection, adding to it by the purchase and exchange of specimens'.

One cannot pretend that Cuming emerges as anything but a rather nebulous character from this hurried sketch. On re-reading the last few pages, however, it is not the ephemeral nature of the sketch that bothers me but the fact that I have been most ill-advised in including the exploits of the man every serious shell collector would emulate alongside my own humble efforts. I have only one valid excuse for doing so, which is the question of atmosphere. Having no details concerning Cuming's expeditions I feel that my notes taken while on the Barrier Reef might fill in some of the gaps.

Let us transport ourselves, then, straight out to Australia, to Bowen on the Queensland coast, one of the small

108 A coloured plate from *Choix de Coquillages et de Crustacées*, by Franz Regenfuss, Copenhagen 1758. The central scallop or *Pecten* is called *Manteau ducal* by Regenfuss. Above and below it are two species of *Murex*

109 (*opposite*) Two examples of the beautiful colouring found in shells: (*top*) *Drupa morum* and (*bottom*) *Coralliophila costularis*

seaports which specialize in chartering boats. It is a gay little place, hot and white, the perfect replica, or was when I was out there in 1947, of one of those towns one has seen depicted in Victorian prints representing newly-founded colonial settlements: a sparseness of buildings gathered down the main street, petering out in a row of wooden shacks; the shacks raised above the ground against white ants. Across the railway, down by a line of coconut palms, we come to the beach and there it is that our boat waits for us, riding impatiently at the end of a long jetty that caterpillars precariously on wooden stilts out into the chalk-blue sea.

I remember the boat well; it was not a graceful clipper but a fifty-foot motor-cruiser called *The Pacific Star*. Being practically flat-bottomed she could stand almost any weather, and had to. I had always imagined the reef

85

110 Searching for shells on the Great Barrier Reef, Queensland, when the coral of the reef is exposed at low tide

111 *Voluta delessertiana*

112 *Voluta concinna*

waters to be glassy smooth and as clear as a crystal lagoon. In point of fact they are neither clear not smooth. The Barrier Reef proper runs in a long line, for some thousand miles or so, thirty to fifty miles off the shore; the intervening channel, the 'Grand Canal' of Australia, is as broad and certainly as rough, if not rougher, than the English Channel. It can be calm of course. My preconceived ideas of the Great Barrier Reef and the North Queensland Coast were wrong in practically every respect. I had imagined it to be tropical, scattered with atolls crowned with palm trees, with corals of course everywhere, their antlered branches and lacy forms prominently displayed. The islands were there in their hundreds but they were not atolls; they rose in wooded peaks more like the steep sides of a Norwegian fjord. The coral lay miles away, out at sea, submerged, except at certain tides, under thirty feet of water, and to get out there in a fifty-foot launch was a tricky job, both the wind and the tides having to be synchronized.

This, however, was not our main concern; in attendance on the tides, we were to cruise around the different islands looking for the beaches and reefs that were known to have shells. People on the North Queensland coast are very shell conscious as, indeed, they well might be. Their lives are littered with molluscs. Every beach one comes to offers its own particular genus; one is known for the spiral cone-shaped trochus, the pretty red and white shell of which buttons are made, a thousand tons of them being shipped annually to the trade; another for a special species of cowries, another for its black and white snails. One

86

113 An engraving of a cone, from the *Tableau Encyclopédique et Méthodique*

114 The coral which forms the Great Barrier Reef. On the right of the photograph can be seen a giant clam wedged into the coral

generally lands on the leeward side of these islands, gliding in one's dinghy through the crystal clear water, the colour of aquamarines, the ripples on the surface moving like clouds across the whiteness of the sand fifteen feet below. Shelving suddenly one bumps to a stop and there in front of one stretches a white crescent-shaped beach fringed with coconut palms, its smoothness disturbed only by the scalloped furrows of a turtle that has dragged its cumbersome shell over the sand to lay its eggs.

I could describe countless beaches but there is one in particular that I remember. The sun was sinking in the late afternoon and in front of us reached a long spit of land, eight or ten miles long, where the sand was as white as snow and as fine as powder. The colours were unbelievably beautiful, the soft colours of eighteenth-century France, fading from rose madder to buff, to the palest blue, a sheen of pearls glowed on the oily waters. The dying sun tinged the sands a pale pink and the bleached shells strewn over its smooth curves, perched on little pedestals worn by the wind, were as fine as paper, piqued and ribbed, pleated like the finest linen. These are the small shells of the Reef.

We move from island to island, spending one morning on the far shore of a wooded peninsula, the haunt of sulphur-crested cockatoos. The beach here faces out towards the Reef and the ocean and its character is quite different. Granite pebbles, polished and smooth as ostrich eggs, take the place of sand while drifts of sea-worn wood and the crushed remains of pearly nautili tell of rough seas. The pebbles are so large that it is hard to walk in one's rope-soled shoes. Off such a beach, out a little way in comparatively deep water, one may hunt for the larger shells; the *Haliotis*, the *Lambis* [figure 125] and the *Melo* [figure 116] as large as a water melon and used by the aborigines for a variety of purposes—as bailers in their log canoes, buckets, saucepans, drinking vessels, baskets and even wardrobes. They represent, perhaps, the only utensil in which a native can boil food, or the sticky glutinous messes which he calls food, usually the intestines of a turtle, all sodden, brought to the boil in salt water.

Shells must be gathered alive if one wants really first-class specimens and in order to obtain them in this state one has to hunt for them; follow their trails, dig in the soft sand, or turn over the rocks. One very soon gets to know their trails, the long straight line of the auger, or

115 The *Turbinella purum* or sacred chank. This specimen is the rare left-handed form of the shell. It is plated in gold and ornamented with rubies and was formerly part of the regalia of the kings of Burma

116 The Baler, or Melon shell, from Australian waters, which is used by the Aborigines for domestic purposes. Specimens may reach eighteen inches in length. From Lovell Reeve's *Conchologia Iconica*

the scroll of the sea snail. Each one leaves its own particular mark. There is no excitement quite like it when turning an old piece of dead coral you suddenly find your first cowry. It is as if you had been given a wonderful present of shiny, smooth porcelain. I defy anyone to spend any length of time on the Reef and remain indifferent. Shells become an obsession. With head bent earthward one wanders on over mile after mile of beach, oblivious to everything except for the few square yards in front of one. It is of no importance how harshly the sun beats down, scorching the back of one's neck; one simply does not notice it, one's major concern being the rocks one has not turned over and the tracks in the sand that have not been excavated. Landscapes change and the light varies, but the most stupendous of sunsets, the most sublime of views are powerless to distract one. The outside world slips by unnoticed. One picks, one scratches and picks again till either one's muscles or one's eyes fail. Only then does one become human again, assuming the upright position so laboriously evolved by man. One winds one's way back to the boat, contented, bearing a tin full of newly acquired treasures, one's neighbour's hoard, if better than one's own, being the only factor that could possibly give one any displeasure.

I remember one afternoon spent in a mangrove swamp, a gloomy world of oozing slime. Gone was the burning sun and the blue sky driven with snowy clouds. The mountains around were covered in mist. Threatening rain clouds completed the dismal scene.

We were ringed round, fenced in, as it were, by the mangroves on their arched stilts which pass as roots, hoop after hoop encrusted with reef oysters, black-lipped, measuring a foot across, growing in clusters. Forcing one open, one finds a mauve, nacreous interior fading off to black. Strange how the colours change from place to place, the sea creatures harmonizing with each other—another example of nature's camouflage. In clear sandy waters one finds the pinks and pale buffs: the clean, faded colours of bright sunlight. Here, amongst the slime and dirt, everything takes on a drabber hue, running the gamut of shades from mauve to purple to inky black. As if conscious of their habitat the creatures in this nether world have all assumed the exaggerated *devil* of Roman Catholicism. The snails are black; crabs too, sheathed in black armour with mauve gauntlets like pall-bearers at

117 The beautifully marked *Oliva porphyria*, a plate from *Coquilles Univalves Marines* by P. L. Duclos, Paris, 1835

118 *Murex palma-rosae*

some medieval funeral. Oysters and mussels, their very nature necessitating them to sport some colour, hide it from view, confining it to their nacreous lining. Black, black—everything is black and grey and evil-smelling—stinking of decay.

Not a day passes on the reef waters without something new being discovered or noticed. One morning whilst roaming amongst the coral, my attention was drawn to a shell that moved over the bottom at an uncommonly fast pace. It was a large trochus and, realizing that all the molluscs familiar to me crawled very slowly, my curiosity was aroused and I picked it up. There was a moment of frantic withdrawal and then out popped the two claws of a hermit crab. It was a large bright red animal with bluish-white spots on its body. I remembered Rumphius complaining of the hermit crabs which deprived him, at night, of the neatly prepared shells lying in his garden for drying. 'This quarrelsome vermin', he writes from Amboyna 'has caused me much grief. I had lain various shells on a raised bank for drying and they climbed on it at night and took away my fine specimens, leaving me their old homes to look at.'

And now comes the problem which confronts every expedition of this nature—how to clean the shells one has laboured so hard to find! The captain of our launch had only a rudimentary knowledge of the procedure and none of us, alas, had thought to inform ourselves. The first week or so, until we obtained proper advice, was just a question of trial and error. Our first haul consisted mainly of the small *Cypraea moneta* [figure 66] with a few large specimens of *Cypraea tigris* and these we just emptied into a saucepan and brought gently to a boil over a fire in the galley. Then, taking the partly cooked shells out with us on to the deck we sat patiently hoiking and rootling about with bent wires, in much the same way as I had seen the Negresses operating at Lamu. The smell was nauseating and lasted for days, even when the shells had been cleaned and emptied. They have a peculiarly insistent odour and smell something like rotten eggs. For several days we worked like this and to combat the smell stuffed plugs of cotton wool soaked in *eau-de-cologne* up our noses. With the bivalves, of course, it was much easier, we placed the creatures in fresh water till they drowned and opened up. This treatment we could not apply to the gasteropods, for although it kills the inhabitants, the creatures always

119 *Telescopium telescopium*, an engraving from Martin Lister's *Historia Conchyliorum*

120 An engraving of *Turritella variegata* from Martin Lister's *Historia Conchyliorum*

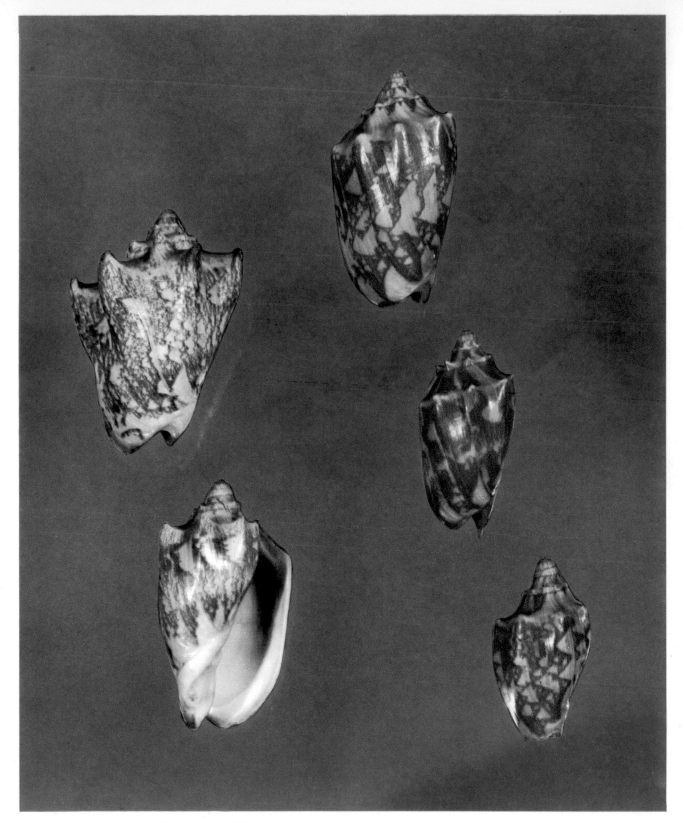

121 Various specimens of *Voluta vespertilio*

contract and withdraw deep within their shells and are impossible to extricate. Some Australian collectors have the habit of burying their shells in dry sand, letting nature take its course, but it is a lengthy procedure and I found that the heat of the sand was apt to dim the sheen on those of the molluscs that possessed it. Of course, it is quite wrong to boil a shell, and even partially boiling them as we did is apt to be dangerous. It can injure or ruin them entirely and specimens which have been prepared in this way will often fade and flake off. No, when I think about it, our encounter with Mrs Jones proved very timely. Mrs Jones was the wife of the Harbour-Master at Bowen, the port from which we set off on our expedition, and the place to which we returned in order to re-fuel. Our captain introduced us since Mrs Jones was reputed to have a most important collection and to be an expert at cleaning. The correct procedure was certainly something quite different to what we had been doing. You place the living shell in salt water to which chloride of sulphate of magnesia has been added; the animals will expand immediately and very soon become stupefied. You must test them and when they no longer withdraw into their shells at your touch, you place them in strong alcohol, or a weak solution of formaldehyde (about eight per cent). This kills the animals while exposed, after which it is easy to extract them from their shells. The shells, of course, should be thoroughly washed after this drastic treatment. Mrs Jones also gave me a few more hints about arranging my collection, warning me against certain cottons, the substance or chemicals in which they have been cleaned being capable of affecting the shells. Rust can also mark them. Examples of this can be seen in Sir Joseph Banks' collection in the British Museum which contains much of the original material from Captain Cook's first voyage round the world. The shells were placed in metal containers made to fit the drawers of the cabinet and contact with the sides of the containers had rusted some of the specimens. I remember also on going through crowded cabinets in different museums finding some of the shells splodged with a kind of white fungus. The patches were rough to the touch as if the shells had come in contact with some acid. This is sometimes called Byne's Disease and nothing very much can be done about it. If caught in time, however, the patches can be washed off with soap and water, taking care to rub the affected parts with some

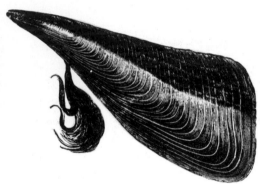

122 The *Pinna*

kind of oil. If left too long the fungus will eventually corrode and discolour the shell. The great Dutch collector, Rumphius, held that one should plunge shells into sea water every two or three years if one wants them to keep their vivid colours.

We talked of many things sitting over a cup of tea on Mrs Jones's latticed veranda. She reminded us how important it is in serious collecting to give the shells their scientific or Latin names. The locality where the shell was obtained is also important. A distant look came into her bespectacled eyes when she told us of her rare finds. After severe storms she had often found shells washed up on the beach and after one particularly bad gale on Lindeman Island, some years ago, she found a reef of bivalves several feet high, stretching along the whole extent of the beach.

Of course, of all the shells one can find on the Reef, the *Tridacna gigas* or giant clam is the one that when first encountered gives one the biggest shock [figure 114]. A pair of shells that would take four or five persons to lift cannot fail to make an impression. The largest specimen known to science measures four feet six inches across while the record weight for a giant clam shell is over half a ton. In Roman Catholic countries they are sometimes used as *bénetiers* or holy water fonts. The interior has a beautiful marble-like appearance and there is a pair like this to be seen in the church of St Sulpice in Paris. They were presented to François I by the Republic of Venice. One would not expect a shell of this size to harbour an animal worth eating, but early voyagers have made reference to its furnishing their sailors with a wholesome meal. Cook assures us that he has seen as many as a dozen men feed off it.

Not even in the most distant past, when gigantic reptiles roamed the earth, did bivalves as large as *Tridacna gigas* exist. This being the case I must be excused for giving a few more details regarding this remarkable shell. It is provided, for instance, with such powerful adductor muscles that when it contracts, the huge shells close like the jaws of a spring trap and can only be forced open by means of a crowbar. There have been cases reported from the Torres Straits of naked pearl divers having been caught by inadvertently placing a foot between the wide-open shells. I have seen several large specimens in shallow water and they are not very easy to distinguish even when

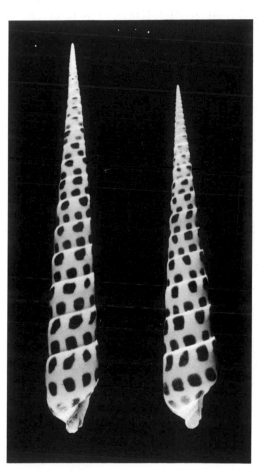

123 *Terebra subulata* from the Great Barrier Reef

open. Their mantles have a velvety appearance and range in colour from brown to olive green and, looking at them, one can easily understand how divers could mistake them for innocent clumps of porite.

Up till now we have been ploughing our way backwards and forwards between the different islands, we have discussed the problems of collecting and cleaning shells; it would seem that the time has come to deal with the Reef proper [figure 110]. It would be frustrating not to include a hurried trip out amongst those uncharted seas. It is a fascinating world, the sea in all its glory—and its cruelty, for unmitigated nature as one finds it out there on the lonely reefs is certainly cruel. It is, an experience no shell collector could forget.

I remember the morning well, it was a bright day mottled with white clouds. The tides were right and the weather forecast promising. At last we had decided to attempt the reefs. The sea, jade green and cobalt, was moderately smooth. Only small waves spanked the sides of the boat, breaking into a spray of silver beads that evaporated the instant they touched the deck, their crystalline sparkle reduced to rings of powdered salt. We had awnings lashed across the bows, but they were powerless against the sun that had burnt us the colour of roasted coffee, and invested the woodwork of our boat with the attributes commonly applied to hot coals, obliging us, if rash enough to forget our shoes, to perform the rites of heathen firewalkers.

It took us five hours to cover the sixty or seventy miles between the islands and the Reef. We read and took pot shots at the large yellow serpents wriggling their leisurely way across the surface of the sea. Bright yellow with dark bands, they littered our way by the dozen, some of them three or four feet long. They will attack, I am told, if one meets them swimming in the water and, like so many of the things up here, are very poisonous. A shoal of porpoise gambolled with us, playing in our wake, their sleek streamlined forms rising up and down, up and down, a kind of effortless perpetual motion out of the water. A giant ray, or a whale, was sighted on the horizon.

When we were only a few miles off the Barrier, the captain mounted the wheelhouse and stood, feet well planted, with a hand shading his eyes on the look-out for the Reef, those tell-tale patches of light water in the

124 *Callanaitis disjecta,* from the Great Barrier Reef

125 (*opposite*) Two specimens of *Lambis rugosa* from the Red Sea

126 and 127 (*below and opposite*) Examples of nature's fantasy: *Columbarium pagoda* from Japan

dark blue sea. 'Proper tiger country this', he remarked as he shouted orders to the engineer below: 'Three points to starboard;' then briskly: 'Knock her to port,' and the water suddenly shallowed, revealing a blur of coral under our bows. 'There's a black head for you.' These black heads are the bane of the Reef. Washed up from the deep by a storm the coral dies and, deposited on top of living organisms, projects above the normal level, forming formidable rocks on which to gash the bottom of your boat. I hate to think what it must be like navigating these waters in a storm at night. With the constant change of the coral, charts are practically useless. The latest charts published by the Admiralty date from 1933 and these are taken mostly from soundings carried out in the last century, hardly likely, with the lapse of some eighty or ninety years, to prove very accurate.

Relaxing his vigil the captain clambered down from his post. 'All right, Archie, cut them out.' The engine slowed down, subsiding from a shuddering roar, dying out with two pathetic little coughs. Anchors were dropped. We had negotiated the passage into a lagoon, or so the crew told us, and we had to take their word for it. None but the initiated would possibly have suspected it. At high tide, with the reefs hidden, it still looked alarmingly like the open sea, vast and lonely, with the wide horizon our only protection.

It was a relief when, towards noon, black heads made their appearance, their glistening crowns drying in the sun. Sheathed in gum boots, wearing bathing suits, shirts and pith helmets, armed with billycans for the shells, we took to the dinghy. The sea changed from blue to aquamarine, then floating over a chasm of green fire; we were on the Reef [figure 110]. When the dinghy scraped the bottom we clambered out, the lukewarm water coming right up over our knees. There we were, literally standing in the sea! It gave one a definite sensation of *malaise*.

How does one set about describing the Great Barrier Reef, this strange sea world teeming with life, created in one of nature's most fantastic moods, coloured more brightly than a rainbow, stained every conceivable hue? It is beautiful, it is sinister, it is a weird world as unfamiliar to us humans as the canals of Mars. It lives at night in the phosphorescent dark, and sleeps by day bathed in brilliant sunshine, the creatures that inhabit it lulled into a sense of false security. At night the coral

flowers and crawling things come out of their shells. It is then that war is waged. Crustacea awake and finny hordes mass for their manœuvres, intent on prey, engaged in the eternal struggle for the survival of the fittest. The whole Reef becomes a giant battlefield; the slaughter is prodigious. Then slowly, slowly, morning dawns, light creeps up over the coral sea and peace reigns once more; the still pools are littered with the panoply of the fray, empty shells and dismembered claws.

One's impressions are hard to describe accurately. One wanders in a trance, hypnotized by what one sees; by the beauty of the colours; the red and mauve coral; yellow staghorns with their antler-like branches hung out in the blue depth of sea, green tipped with blue, pink and green, the bright pinks and greens of heraldry; the cinnamon, lavender, russet and grey of the porites sprawled out in clumps like a herbaceous border. One finds polyps, coral with gills like a mushroom and anemones that measure a foot across, resembling chrysanthemums, their petals waving in the currents as if stirred by a faint autumn breeze. Bedded among the corals are the horseshoe clams with their incredible mantles of emerald and sapphire or cool greens and russet browns that retract as you touch them, squirting water at you as they clamp shut their scalloped shells. Their squirts can be heard all round you as they eject unwanted particles of food, breaking the dead stillness. In a sunny pool free from coral, one finds blue starfish, lapis-lazuli blue, that, instead of swallowing their food, eject a baggy stomach with which they envelop their prey, digesting it before it is drawn back again. There are black starfish with arms jointed like a necklace, beads of jet edged round with ostrich feathers. There are starfish with writhing tentacles like centipedes, and sea worms armed with a thousand glassy spines that can penetrate the thickest leather glove. There are vermilion crabs spotted with white like toadstools, mauve coral crabs, mottled rock crabs, and lobsters that have taken upon themselves every colour of the Reef, blue, mauve, purple, green, orange, brown, red and black, broken by spots on the various parts of the body and stripes along the legs. Occasionally you will find the giant spider crabs of Japanese waters that can measure up to twelve feet across their outstretched limbs, stilted horrors that stalk each other at night across the beaches. Farther out to sea they have fifty-foot squids, but these monsters are not common.

Care has to be exercised, however, to avoid the smaller but infinitely more poisonous creatures; the coneshell and the dreaded stone-fish. Both are common on the Reef and both have been known to kill people.

Time passes quickly out here on the reefs. We had started off in a little group of six, we were now scattered in every direction, dwindled to little specks on the sea. One gets carried away, each step bringing some new curiosity; sea hares like enormous snails without a shell that hide themselves in clouds of sepia ink, or a yellow and black-banded lamprey stranded in the shallow water looking like a baby shark. The fishes are beyond number, as brightly coloured as the corals among which they live.

For hours we wandered as though lost in a dream. The tide was rising and it was time we returned to the ship. There we sat after dinner on deck, the six of us, silenced by what we had seen. Frightened too; it is so lonely out here in the world of shells and sea creatures. It is with fear that I remember wading across the reefs in my boots. Suddenly one looks up and there one is alone, stranded in an immensity of ocean, walking the seas. Nothing, nothing—all is nothingness. No one had told me this about the Reef and yet my most vivid impression of it is this sensation of fear, a cold impersonal fear.

The Great Barrier Reef is a living museum, where any visitor may acquire for himself some of the greatest treasures in the conchological world. There is much enjoyment to be derived from assembling a collection of shells from other people's discoveries: but nothing can touch the enjoyment of searching and finding for oneself, in treasure-houses like the Reef, these extraordinary, beautiful and sometimes even savage artifices of nature.